MW01701526

When Children Refuse School

A Cognitive-Behavioral Therapy Approach

Parent Workbook

Christopher A. Kearney
Anne Marie Albano

TherapyWorks
The Psychological Corporation

Printed in the United States of America.

1 2 3 4 5 6 7 8 9 10 11 12 A B C D E

About the Authors

CHRISTOPHER A. KEARNEY, PhD, is an associate professor of clinical child psychology at the University of Nevada, Las Vegas. He is also the director of the UNLV Child School Refusal and Anxiety Disorders Clinic. Dr. Kearney received his BA from the State University of New York at Binghamton and his MA and PhD from the State University of New York at Albany. He completed his internship at the University of Mississippi Medical Center. Dr. Kearney's research has focused primarily on the classification, assessment, and treatment of school refusal behavior and internalizing disorders in children and adolescents. He also works with adults with severe developmental disabilities. Dr. Kearney has served in editorial positions for the *Journal of Clinical Child Psychology* and *Behavior Therapy*. Dr. Kearney has co-authored and co-edited two books on anxiety disorders in youth, authored a casebook on childhood behavior disorders and a book on school refusal behavior, and written numerous journal articles and book chapters. He is the recipient of the Barrick Scholar Award, the William Morris Award for Excellence in Scholarship, and the Distinguished Teaching Award from the University of Nevada, Las Vegas.

ANNE MARIE ALBANO, PhD, is an assistant professor of psychiatry and director of the Anxiety Disorders Clinical Research Service at the Child Study Center of New York University Medical Center. She has held positions as an assistant professor of psychology at the University of Louisville, and as assistant director of the Phobia and Anxiety Disorders Clinic of the State University of New York at Albany. Dr. Albano received her PhD from the University of Mississippi and completed a postdoctoral fellowship at the SUNY Phobia Clinic. Dr. Albano has served in editorial positions for *Cognitive and Behavioral Practice*, and serves on the editorial boards of several journals. She is the former Chair of the Continuing Education Issues Committee for AABT. Dr. Albano and Dr. Wendy Silverman have co-authored the *Anxiety Disorders Interview Schedule for DSM-IV*, child and parent versions. Her main clinical and research interests are in the development and dissemination of empirically supported assessment and treatment protocols for youth. In addition to school refusal, she and her colleagues have developed cognitive behavioral treatment programs for social phobia, obsessive compulsive disorder, and mixed anxiety and depression.

Acknowledgments

We sincerely thank our mentors, students, colleagues, and the children and parents we have seen who have helped us develop this workbook and treatment procedures over the past several years. Special thanks go out to Drs. Wendy K. Silverman and David H. Barlow for their significant support and feedback. Dr. Kearney also wishes to thank his wife, Kimberlie, for her emotional support during the phases of this project.

We would also like to thank the various individuals at The Psychological Corporation for their efforts and contributions. As project director, Sandra Prince-Embury, PhD, has coordinated the development of the parent workbook and contributed significantly to its expression in a form that is helpful to parents. Appreciation is also extended to those persons whose diligent and meticulous efforts were essential in preparing the parent workbook. Among these individuals are: Stephanie Tong, MA, Anthony Weyer, MA, and Jennifer Brown, research assistants; Kathy Overstreet, senior editor, Elizabeth Manclark, editor, and Janice Miller, PhD, editor; Marian Zahora, designer; Cynthia Sweet, production specialist; Robin Espiritu, manufacturing specialist; and Javier Flores, associate designer. Special appreciation is extended to Aurelio Prifitera, PhD, president of the Clinical Division, and to Larry Weiss, PhD, director of the Behavioral Health Care and Personality Group.

Contents

Introduction

This parent workbook is designed to help you work with a qualified therapist to resolve your child's school refusal behavior. The workbook defines school refusal behavior, describes how your situation might be evaluated, and shows what you and a therapist can do so that your child is able to attend school without distress. You should use this workbook with a qualified therapist who is concurrently using the therapist guide to treat your child's school refusal behavior.

What is School Refusal Behavior?

School refusal behavior refers to children aged 5–17 years who refuse to attend school and/or have trouble remaining in classes for an entire day. School refusal behavior is a difficult and widespread problem, and can develop into a more serious one if left untreated. Specifically, your child may show school refusal behavior if he or she:

- does not attend school at all, and/or
- goes to school but then leaves school during the course of the day, and/or
- goes to school but only after behavior problems in the morning, such as throwing temper tantrums or refusing to move, and/or
- has an unusually high degree of distress about going to school and begs you or your spouse not to make him or her go back to school.

School refusal behavior is thus pertinent to many different children, including those who always miss school as well as those who rarely miss school but attend while experiencing a high degree of distress. School refusal behavior is also defined by the length of time the problem has lasted. *Acute school refusal behavior* refers to cases lasting two weeks to one calendar year, having been a problem for a majority of that time. *Chronic school refusal behavior* refers to cases lasting longer than one calendar year, or across two academic years, having been a problem for a majority of that time. School refusal behavior, as defined in this workbook, may not include cases that involve one or more of the following:

- legitimate physical illness (e.g., asthma) that makes school attendance difficult,
- school withdrawal, when a parent deliberately keeps a child home from school,
- social or familial conditions that predominate a child's life (e.g., homelessness, running away to avoid abuse),
- other problems that are more substantial than school refusal behavior (e.g., poor schoolwork, depression, overactivity, aggression, general lack of motivation).

If any of these circumstances applies to your situation, then the procedures described in this workbook may not be appropriate for your child.

Frequency and Major Features of School Refusal Behavior

School refusal behavior is a common problem among American children and adolescents, affecting as many as 28%. The problem occurs equally among boys and girls. Most children with school refusal behavior are aged 10–13 years, but the problem also peaks at ages 5–6 and 14–15 years as children enter new schools. However, children may show school refusal behavior anytime between ages 5 and 17 years.

Many different behaviors are shown by children with school refusal behavior. These behaviors fall into two groups. The first group of school refusal behaviors are those that are less obvious. Common examples include general anxiety, social anxiety and withdrawal, depression, fear, and physical symptoms (especially stomachaches, headaches, nausea, and tremors). The second group of school refusal behaviors are those that are more obvious. Common examples include tantrums (including crying, screaming, flailing of limbs), verbal and physical aggression, reassurance-seeking, clinging, refusal to move, noncompliance, and running away from school or home.

If nothing is done about school refusal behavior, serious problems could develop. In the short-term, a child could experience more trouble with schoolwork, poor grades, and alienation from friends. In addition, the child's family might experience conflict, disruption in their daily routine, and legal problems. In the long-term, a child with school refusal behavior might have trouble getting into college, have occupational and marital problems, and show alcohol abuse, criminal behavior, and anxiety and depression. Of course, not all children will experience these problems, but the chances of these problems developing are greater as a child misses more and more school.

Reasons for School Refusal Behavior

Although children show many different school refusal behaviors, the reasons for these behaviors may be few. Clinical research indicates that children refuse school for one or more of the following reasons:

- to avoid objects or situations that make the child feel unpleasant physical symptoms or general distress (negative affect).
- to escape social and/or evaluative situations that are painful to the child.
- to receive attention from a parent or significant other.
- to pursue tangible rewards outside of school that make skipping school more fun than staying in school.

The first two reasons refer to children who refuse school to get away from something negative. Common examples of school-related *objects* or *situations* that children sometimes avoid are buses, fire alarms, gymnasiums, playgrounds, hallways, and classroom items. Common examples of school-related *social situations* that children sometimes avoid are interactions with peers, teachers, principals, and children who are verbally or physically aggressive. Common examples of school-related *evaluative situations* that children sometimes avoid are tests, recitals, athletic performances, and speaking or writing in front of others. Remember that children often refuse school for both of these first two reasons.

The second two reasons refer to children who refuse school to get something positive outside of school. For example, younger children sometimes refuse school so their parents will stay close and give them extra attention. Older children and adolescents sometimes refuse school to engage in specific activities such as watching television at home, engaging in social parties with friends, and using alcohol or other drugs.

Children sometimes refuse school for two or more of the reasons listed above. For example, some children are initially anxious about school activities and try to remain home to stay away from them. These children may then discover the many interesting things they can do at home during the day. Therefore, they refuse school to stay away from something at school *and* to obtain tangible rewards outside of school. Some children miss school for long periods to be with their friends, but then cannot face the difficult prospect of having to return to school and adjust to new classes, teachers, and peers.

Children who refuse school for two or more reasons will probably need more than one treatment, and treatment for a longer period of time, compared to children who refuse school for one reason. In addition, children out of school for long periods of time will probably need longer and more intense treatment than children out of school for shorter periods of time. Because children often refuse school for more than one reason, you should read all the parts of this workbook that are relevant to your family's situation.

Traditional Treatments for School Refusal Behavior

Because school refusal behavior is a serious problem, mental health professionals and educators have tried to treat it in different ways. Some common ways include:

- increasing the physical and emotional distance between the parent and child to reduce separation problems.
- increasing the child's self-esteem in the classroom.
- teaching the child to relax so he or she can cope with an object or situation at school that makes him or her upset.
- forcing the child to go to school.
- negotiating a solution to the school refusal problem among family members.
- medicating the child using antidepressant or antianxiety drugs.
- placing the child in an inpatient residential program.

In general, each of these treatments works well for some, but not all, children with school refusal behavior. For example, increasing parent-child distance or forcing a child to attend school may work well for young children but not adolescents. Teaching a child to relax may work well for those who are fearful but less well for those who are not fearful during school. Other treatments, such as family therapy, require verbal input that might be difficult for young children. Medication works well for some children but not others, and side effects are sometimes a problem. Finally, inpatient treatment is sometimes recommended for chronic, but not acute, cases of school refusal behavior.

A New Model for Addressing Children With School Refusal Behavior

Because traditional treatments do not work for all children, this workbook presents a new model that divides school refusal behavior into different groups. These groups are based on the four reasons why children refuse school. Specific treatments are then given on the basis of the group most relevant to a child. This model has been shown to be more effective than using just one treatment for all children with school refusal behavior.

Chapter 2 of this workbook describes how a child with school refusal behavior is assigned to one of these four groups. After this assignment, a specific treatment is given. A different treatment is used for each group. If a child's behavior falls into more than one group, then more than one treatment is used. Overall, this may the best way of changing different school refusal behaviors. The specific treatments are:

- For children who refuse school to avoid objects or situations that cause general distress, treatment helps them control their excess physical symptoms and gradually reintroduces them to their regular classroom.
- For children who refuse school to escape painful social and/or evaluative situations, treatment helps them build social/coping skills and reduce their social anxiety.
- For children who refuse school for attention, treatment uses parent-based techniques to increase parent control, change parent commands, establish routines, and set up rewards for school attendance and punishments for school refusal behavior.
- For children who refuse school to pursue tangible rewards outside of school, treatment uses family-based techniques to increase rewards for school attendance, curtail the child's activities for nonattendance, and provide the family and child with problem-solving strategies to reduce conflict and other difficulties.

Does This Workbook Fit Your Child?

Because school refusal behavior is often caused by various problems, it may be difficult for you to know whether this workbook is appropriate for your child. This section provides some sample questions that a therapist may ask you when you first speak with him or her. Your answers should tell you and the therapist if this workbook will be useful.

Has your child just started refusing to go to school?

Your answer to this question may be important in deciding whether to go any further in assessment or treatment. If your child's school refusal behavior has lasted less than two weeks, there is still an excellent chance that it will end on its own. In this case, the therapist may suggest that you call back in one week if the problem persists or schedule an appointment for one week later. In many cases, this appointment turns out to be unnecessary because the child has returned to school on his or her own.

On the other hand, the therapist may recommend that you come in for assessment if your child's school refusal behavior has been occurring every day for at least one week and is severe enough that it leads to serious family fighting or disruption in your family's daily routine. In this case, or if your child has been refusing school for more than two weeks, an assessment session would probably be appropriate.

What is your child's most serious behavior problem?

Although this question may be difficult to answer, try to think about whether your child shows behaviors that are more serious than his or her school refusal behavior. Ask yourself, for example, whether your child:

- is afraid to leave you or the house for any reason, not just to go to school.
- is sad or unmotivated in many situations, not just those involving school.
- has expressed recent thoughts about harming himself or herself.
- is more overactive in all situations compared to most children his or her age.
- is failing school, but not because of school refusal behavior.
- refuses to do what you ask in all situations, not just those related to school.
- uses alcohol or other drugs on a regular basis.
- steals or destroys property on a regular basis.
- is frequently aggressive toward others.

If you think that these or other behaviors are more serious than school refusal, then this workbook may be only partially useful. It may be partially useful because changing school refusal behavior can be the first step toward resolving other problems. For example, a parent may have a child who does not listen to commands and is "out of control." Although these are real problems, many parents want to focus first on school refusal behavior because it is more urgent and because it can lead to improvement in the other behaviors. In cases where the first step in treating other problems is returning a child to school, the treatments described in this workbook may be helpful.

However, you may feel "in the dark" or confused and upset by your child's problems. As a result, you may not know which of your child's behaviors is the most serious. Try to give the therapist as much information as possible about your child's different behaviors. When doing so, try to avoid a common mistake that some parents make. Some parents pay more attention to obvious behaviors, such as breaking curfew or not doing homework, and pay less attention to signs of anxiety or depression. Try to give the therapist information about all relevant behaviors, even those that are harder to identify. It may be helpful to contact others, such as your child's teachers, who might provide additional information.

What extenuating circumstances might be causing your child's school refusal behavior?

In many cases of school refusal behavior, extenuating circumstances may explain the problem. For example, the therapist may want to know about your child's medical problems. Often, school refusal behavior is related to problems such as asthma, pain, insomnia, diabetes, infection, or physical handicap. If you think this is possible, then your child should first see a pediatrician for a medical examination. In addition, you and the therapist (with your permission) should consult a medical doctor as necessary and appropriate throughout therapy.

Examples of extenuating circumstances are when parents keep a child home from school for economic reasons, or as a safety person to help with a parent's own anxiety problem, or out of fear that the child will be kidnapped. In other cases, more serious family problems, such as sexual abuse, may apply. If circumstances such as these exist, then discuss them with the therapist. Many families hold back important information out of embarrassment or fear. However, it is important for the therapist to have this information so that he or she can develop the best treatment plan for you and your child.

What is your child's age?

The therapist will likely ask your child's age. This information is important because the treatments described in this workbook have been specifically designed for children aged 5–17 years. They were not designed for children younger than 5 years who may be refusing to attend preschool or day care. Also, knowing your child's age will help the therapist plan the best assessment and treatment for your child. For example, treatments that rely heavily on verbal discussion may be more appropriate for adolescents than young children. On the other hand, physically bringing a 6-year-old child to school is much easier than bringing a 16-year-old adolescent.

Is your child's school refusal behavior extremely severe?

The treatments described in this workbook may not fit extremely severe cases of school refusal behavior. Extremely severe cases show very high levels of distress, substantial delinquent behavior, school absence longer than two years, and other behaviors. In these cases, other treatments will probably be necessary before, or in addition to, the ones described here. Examples of other treatments include drug therapy for extreme anxiety, residential or inpatient treatment for substantial delinquent behavior, or alternative school programs for extended absence. Be sure to talk with the therapist about alternative treatments that may be best for your child.

What if This Workbook Does Not Fit Your Child?

If you are not sure whether.this workbook fits your child, then discuss your situation with a knowledgeable therapist. The therapist should be able to tell you if the procedures described here and in the therapist guide will be helpful. If necessary, the therapist can refer you to another therapist who specializes in your child's problem. Remember, the procedures described in this workbook are designed specifically for children whose school refusal behavior is their major problem.

What Benefits Will You Receive From Reading This Workbook?

This workbook is written to help you understand the procedures that may take place during assessment and treatment of your child's school refusal behavior, and to address questions that you may have about the process. By increasing your understanding of these procedures, you will become an active participant in your child's assessment and treatment. *The procedures described in this workbook work very well if parents and family members follow through with what needs to be done.* This workbook describes a clear, step-by-step process to help you work with the therapist.

As you use this workbook with a therapist, thoroughly reread each section (e.g., Session 1) *before* each individual session with the therapist. Become familiar with the main points of each section and write down a list of the major points that will be covered in the session. Write down any questions or concerns you have at this time or in the future. Review these with the therapist whenever possible.

The procedures described in this workbook are based on clinical experience and have been tested for various problems. However, these procedures are meant for *typical* cases of school refusal behavior. As a result, you may find that some changes will have to be made for your child. Unforeseen circumstances always arise, and therefore the treatment procedures are flexible. You will also need to be flexible when working with your child's therapist. For example, some cases of school refusal behavior take less time to resolve than what is described in this workbook. Other cases take more time. This workbook is a guide only.

The Structure of This Parent Workbook

This workbook provides you with an outline of what to expect if a therapist uses these procedures to treat your child's school refusal behavior. Chapter 2 describes what to expect in an assessment session and how you can help the therapist monitor your child's behavior. Chapter 3 describes what to expect in consultation and treatment sessions. Chapters 4–7 describe treatments for each type of school refusal behavior and include sample dialogues and troubleshooting recommendations. Finally, Chapter 8 describes how to prevent problems in the future. Appendix A contains figures that are applicable to multiple treatments. Figures may be photocopied for convenience.

Assessment

This chapter describes the assessment process for children with school refusal behavior and includes the purpose and methods of assessment, monitoring daily progress, contacting school officials, and other information. A brief sample case is also provided.

What is Assessment and What is its Purpose?

Assessment refers to the ways in which the therapist will gather information about your child. The therapist sets up an assessment session to better understand you, your child, and the school refusal behavior. At the beginning of the session, the therapist will inform you and your child that most information you give is *confidential* (the therapist will outline exceptions for you). The therapist will not give the information to anyone else unless you give permission. You may be asked to read and sign a consent form that describes the upcoming procedures. The consent form also allows the therapist to speak with others who can help, such as school officials. The therapist will probably want to see you and your child separately during the assessment session, to let each of you talk more freely.

Although some things you talk about will be sensitive, you, your spouse (if you have one), and your child should be as honest as possible so that the therapist can learn answers to three basic questions:

- What is your child's major behavior problem?
- What is maintaining his or her school refusal behavior?
- What is the best treatment for your child?

To answer these questions, the therapist will need to know exactly which school refusal behaviors are present. For example, he or she might ask about your child's school avoidance, ways of thinking, or physical symptoms. The therapist will need to know how often your child is attending school and his or her history of school refusal behavior over the past days, weeks, and months. The therapist will also try to understand why your child is continuing to refuse school. To do this, he or she may ask questions about how your child is rewarded for being out of school, how school refusal might be influenced by you or other family members, and how you or your spouse respond when your child refuses school.

During assessment, the therapist will also want to understand your family's ways of interacting, your parenting style, and your child's personality, social relationships, school achievement, and related problems. The therapist may also ask about other things and will gather information about other concerns you may have. These discussions with the therapist may sometimes be uncomfortable, but they will help the therapist better understand your situation and design a good treatment plan. These assessment discussions will also help you and your child develop a positive relationship with the therapist that is crucial for later therapy.

What Will Happen During Assessment?

None of the assessment procedures is threatening, but some sensitive areas may be covered. The therapist will use some basic procedures, including interviews and questionnaires. The therapist may also want to observe your child as he or she attempts to go to school. Remember that you can choose to decline any question or procedure and ask any question during assessment.

The Interview

When assessing a behavior problem, most therapists use some type of interview. Different therapists use different interviews and interviewing styles. The questions they ask will vary, depending on the case they are assessing. However, to prepare you for what might be asked, some likely and pertinent questions are presented here:

How often does your child refuse school *specifically* because he or she wants to avoid objects or situations that cause general distress? The therapist might also ask some follow-up questions:

- Is your child more distressed about school than most children his or her age?
- Are there specific school-related objects or situations that he or she wants to avoid?
- Has your child told you of recent negative life events, or have you noticed that he or she has suddenly changed his or her behavior in any way?
- Has your child expressed to you or have you noticed any specific emotions or physical symptoms about going to school? What are they?
- Do these problems occur every day or primarily on school days?

How often does your child refuse school *specifically* because he or she wants to escape painful social and/or evaluative situations? Follow-up questions:

- Does your child try to escape these situations more than most children his or her age?
- Are there specific social and/or evaluative situations that he or she prefers to stay away from (especially writing or speaking in front of others, meeting new people, interacting with aggressive peers, performing during recitals, tests, or athletic contests, or being in or approaching large groups of people)?
- Has your child told you of recent negative social or evaluative events, or have you noticed that he or she has suddenly changed his or her social behavior in any way?
- Has your child expressed to you or have you noticed any specific emotions or physical symptoms about interacting in social or evaluative situations? What are they?
- Do these problems occur in all social or evaluative situations or primarily in school-related situations?

How often does your child refuse school *specifically* because he or she wants attention from you or a significant other? Follow-up questions:

- Does your child show this attention-seeking behavior more than most children his or her age?
- Are there specific behaviors that your child engages in to get attention from you (especially clinging, reassurance-seeking, refusal to move, tantrums, telephone calling, protests, verbal demands for attention, guilt-inducing behavior, or running away from school to get to you)?
- Has your child told you of recent negative life events, or have you noticed that he or she has suddenly changed his or her behavior toward you in any way?
- Has your child expressed to you or have you noticed any specific emotions or physical symptoms about interacting with you or being away from you? What are they?
- Do these problems occur in most daily-life situations or primarily in school-related situations?

How often does your child refuse school *specifically* because he or she wants to pursue tangible rewards from some source outside of school? Follow-up questions:

- Does your child pursue tangible rewards outside of school more than most children his or her age?
- Are there specific rewards that your child leaves school to pursue (especially spending time with friends, alcohol/drug use, watching television or playing

games at home, riding a bicycle, sleeping, or attending shopping centers or casinos)?

- Has your child told you of recent negative life or school events, or have you noticed that he or she has suddenly changed his or her behavior in any way?
- Has your child expressed to you or have you noticed any specific emotions or physical symptoms about being in or leaving school? What are they?
- Does your child pursue rewards in many daily-life situations or primarily when school is in session?

Does your child refuse school for a combination of the reasons just discussed? If so, which ones do you feel are most important?

Remember that these questions will not be the only ones asked by the therapist. Other behaviors may need to be assessed and other information may be needed. Also, remember that you may add as much information to the interview as you like. In general, the more information you give, the better. In addition, if the therapist does not ask some of the questions listed here, feel free to raise them yourself and provide answers if possible in the assessment session.

Questionnaires

The therapist may also ask your child to fill out some questionnaires. Questionnaires are often used to gather additional and more specific kinds of information than what the therapist gathered during the interview. For example, some questionnaires your child completes might evaluate his or her levels of general and social anxiety, depression, fear, self-esteem, and enjoyment of school. Other questionnaires might examine your child's acting-out behavior. You and your child should read the questionnaires before agreeing to fill them out.

The therapist may ask you to complete some questionnaires as well. Parent questionnaires, for example, might focus on your child's behavior, your marital relationship, and family interactions. Read the questionnaires before agreeing to fill them out. The therapist may also obtain, with your permission, a questionnaire from your child's teacher about social, academic, and behavioral problems that your child may be having at school.

A key questionnaire that the therapist may ask you to complete is the School Refusal Assessment Scale (SRAS). The SRAS helps identify the major reasons why a child is refusing school. There are separate versions of the questionnaire for children and parents (see Figures A.1 and A.2). Be as honest as possible when completing these questionnaires.

Observation

If possible, the therapist will directly observe your child's and family's morning activities. This observation might give the therapist additional information and help him or her better understand why your child is continuing to refuse school. The therapist will want to observe your child's and family's behaviors under different circumstances.

What if you think your child refuses school to avoid objects or situations that cause general distress? In this case, it may be useful for the therapist to compare your child's behavior when asked to attend school under *regular* circumstances with your child's behavior:

- when asked to attend school under different circumstances (e.g., no full-day attendance, physical education class, lunch with peers, or playground), or
- when asked to go with you to an equally large building that resembles a school (e.g., an office building with similar busy activity).

What if you think your child refuses school to escape painful social and/or evaluative situations? In this case, it may be useful for the therapist to compare your child's behavior when asked to attend school under *regular* circumstances with your child's behavior:

- when asked to attend school under different circumstances (e.g., no recitals, oral presentations, athletic performances, or intense social interactions), or
- when asked to go to the school building when classes are not in session (i.e., with no one or just a few people present).

What if you think your child refuses school for attention? In this case, it may be useful for the therapist to compare your child's behavior when asked to attend school under *regular* circumstances with your child's behavior when:

- you go with your child to school and the classroom, or
- your child is allowed to contact you at any time during the school day and be picked up from school by you (or your spouse).

What if you think your child refuses school to pursue tangible rewards outside of school? In this case, it may be useful for the therapist to compare your child's behavior when asked to attend school under *regular* circumstances with your child's behavior when:

- more rewards are made available for attending school, or
- your child's fun activities are reduced when he or she misses school.

The therapist will look to see if your child changes his or her behavior under different circumstances. Specifically, the therapist will watch for:

- clinging, refusal to move, running away, and/or not listening to parent requests or commands.
- physical reactions such as stomachaches, headaches, abdominal pain, tremors, and nausea/vomiting.
- complaints about discomfort related to school.
- sudden changes in behavior.
- pleas to end the observation and return home.
- your reactions and family members' reactions to your child's behavior.
- teacher reports of your child's behavior at school.

What is the Best Treatment for Your Child?

By the end of assessment, you and the therapist should understand your child's major school refusal behaviors and why they continue to occur. Based on this assessment, the therapist will form a treatment plan for your case. In this model of school refusal behavior, different treatments are based on why a child refuses school:

- If your child refuses school to avoid objects or situations that lead to general distress, recommended treatment focuses on reducing physical symptoms and avoidance of school.
- If your child refuses school to escape painful social and/or evaluative situations, recommended treatment focuses on building social/coping skills and reducing social anxiety.
- If your child refuses school for attention, recommended treatment focuses on improving parent commands, routines, and methods of discipline to shift attention toward school attendance behavior and away from school refusal behavior.
- If your child refuses school to pursue tangible rewards outside of school, recommended treatment focuses on improving your family's ability to negotiate solutions to problems, increasing rewards for attending school, and decreasing rewards for missing school.

If your child refuses school for two or more of these reasons, a combination of these treatments is recommended. These treatments are described in detail in Chapters 4–7 of this workbook.

Monitoring School Refusal Behavior on a Daily Basis

The therapist may also ask you and your child to keep track of school refusal behavior and school attendance on a daily basis. This will help you and your child better understand changes in your child's behavior over time. Also, you and your child will not need to rely so much on memory when you talk to the therapist. The information you give will also help the therapist understand your current situation and adjust treatment as necessary. In addition, changes in behavior over time may be used to chart improvement.

The therapist may also ask you and your child to give ratings on daily logbooks (see Figures A.3 and A.4). *Child and parent logbooks should be kept separately.* Be careful not to influence your child's ratings, but remind him or her to complete the form each day. If your child has a question about what rating to give, have him or her contact the therapist as soon as possible.

Ratings are made using a 0–10 scale ranging from 0 (*none*) to 10 (*extreme amount*). Ratings may be made about your child's anxiety (nervousness, tension), depression (sadness, unhappiness), and general distress (general feelings of dread or being upset). In addition, you may rate your child's noncompliance (not listening to parent commands) and disruption of your family's daily routine. You might also chart your child's behavior problems and time missed from school. *Finally, if you think that any event is important for the therapist to know, write it down on the front or back of the logbook.*

The therapist will show you and your child how to complete the logbooks. He or she may show you a sample of a completed logbook to explain how it is scored. You and your child should complete the logbooks each evening, after most of the day has passed. Be sure to ask the therapist any questions you or your child have about the logbooks before you leave the assessment session. Also, contact the therapist should any questions arise over the next few days.

These logbooks are vital for the therapist to get a clear picture of what is happening at home and school. They are also vital for you to better understand the patterns of your child's behavior. *Therefore, it is extremely important that you and your child complete these logbooks daily and bring them to each session.* This includes the next session, called the consultation session, which is usually scheduled 5–7 days after the formal assessment session.

Contacting School Officials

It will be helpful if you let the therapist contact school officials for additional information, but this is not a requirement. Helpful school officials may be teachers (including specialized ones such as physical education teachers), school psychologists, counselors, principals, nurses, librarians, or other staff members. You and the therapist should maintain contact with these officials throughout the course of treatment. Important information from school officials might include:

- course schedules, grades, written work, and required make-up work.
- goals and attitudes of school officials and peers regarding your child.
- procedures and timelines for getting your child back into school.
- potential obstacles to getting your child back into school.
- past school refusal behavior.
- general social or other behaviors of your child in school.
- map of the school (e.g., lockers, cafeteria, library, etc.).
- feedback about the effectiveness of the treatment procedures.
- disciplinary and related procedures.
- rules about absenteeism, conduct, or leaving school areas.
- alternative school programs.
- advice that school officials have previously given you regarding your child's school refusal behavior (e.g., forcibly bring your child to school; place him or her in home schooling or on drug therapy).

If you have experienced conflict with school officials, be sure to tell the therapist. Although such conflict is not unusual, keep in mind that cooperation from school officials is often crucial for changing a child's school refusal behavior. For example, helpful school officials are often essential for reintegrating a child into school and for keeping him or her there. You should allow the therapist to act as a mediator between yourself and school officials if necessary. In addition, you should work to repair your relationships with school officials now and throughout the course of therapy.

Contacting Medical Professionals

The therapist may also ask your permission to speak with your child's pediatrician or other medical professionals who are currently treating your child or who have done so in the past. The procedures described in this workbook may need to be altered if your child has certain medical conditions (e.g., asthma, pain). Be sure to have a thorough discussion with the therapist about all of the pertinent medical conditions that affect your child.

A Sample Case of Assessment and Assigning Treatment

Here is a brief sample case of a 9-year-old boy who had difficulties going to school for three months. His behaviors included crying, clinging, pleas for nonattendance, and running out of the classroom. These problems became worse over time, and the child had not been in school for four weeks. His parents referred him for treatment and were afraid to force him to go to school. In the meantime, during the day, the boy played games with his mother, watched television, and rode his bicycle around the neighborhood.

An assessment using an interview, questionnaires, and therapist observation showed that the boy was refusing school for both attention and because it was more fun to be out of school. The child said he was willing to attend school if he knew his mother was sitting in the main office and if he could contact her whenever he wanted. This was not the case if the therapist was at school instead of his mother. In addition, the child increased his tantrums when not allowed to continue his daily fun activities. Therefore, two treatments were recommended: parent training to reduce attention for school refusal behavior, and contracting between the child and parents to increase rewards for going to school and decrease rewards for missing school.

Consultation Session and General Procedures

In this chapter you will learn about what may happen during a consultation session and some general procedures regarding treatment sessions. In a consultation session, the therapist usually summarizes assessment results and provides recommendations to your family about treatment.

The Consultation Session

Discussion of the Past Week

The therapist will probably want to speak with you and your child separately for at least part of the time. He or she will remind everyone about confidentiality and ask about family life since the last session. Be sure to give the therapist any new information about sudden changes in behavior. Be specific about how much time your child missed from school, his or her distress and acting-out behaviors, how you responded to your child's school refusal behavior, important school and home activities, and family interactions.

If much change has occurred in your child's school refusal behavior since the last session, then the therapist may re-interview you or your child and/or readminister some questionnaires or other procedures. This will be done to see if any changes in the treatment plan are needed. If little change occurred since the last session, then the therapist will move on to the next step.

Discussion of Daily Logbooks

The therapist will examine your daily logbook ratings for two main reasons. First, he or she will see if the logbooks were brought in and completed properly. If you had problems, the therapist will discuss these with you and your child. Common problems include forgetfulness, lack of motivation, or confusion about how to complete the logbooks. *These issues must be resolved immediately.* If you or your child had any problems completing the logbooks, discuss these problems with the therapist now.

Second, the therapist will be interested in any trends in anxiety, depression, distress, noncompliance, or disruption of the family. For example, some children with school refusal behavior show particularly severe anxiety ratings on Sunday and Monday nights as the new school week starts. This may indicate where treatment will have to be focused at some point. The therapist will also note any discrepancies in the logbooks, read written comments made on the logbooks, and check for sudden changes in behavior during the week.

Discussion of Assessment Results

Following a discussion of the logbooks, the therapist will discuss the assessment results with you and your child. The therapist may include:

- information from interviews and information regarding diagnosis.
- information from questionnaires or formal tests.
- information from observations.
- differences between child and parent reports.
- teacher or school official/academic reports.
- other information obtained from other sources (e.g., medical doctor).
- other information deemed relevant by the therapist that may impact upon your case (e.g., crises, family members, individual perspectives, history, environment, interpersonal relationships, current stressors and resources).

Following this discussion, the therapist will provide answers to your questions and describe what he or she thinks are your child's major school refusal behaviors, what he or she believes is maintaining school refusal behavior, and a general outline of treatment goals, expected outcome, and timeline.

As the therapist discusses these things, be sure to add information or raise any disagreements you may have. Feel free to ask questions and take notes if you like. *Most importantly, try to be open-minded about what the therapist is saying.* Some parents and children find it difficult to accept that they will have to change some of their behavior. However, you or other family members may need to be a major focus of treatment. As a result, the therapist will try to explain why a specific treatment plan was chosen.

Providing a Rationale for Treatment

After summarizing the assessment results, the therapist will discuss why he or she recommends a certain treatment for your family. In addition, the therapist will describe each aspect of recommended treatment.

If your child is refusing school to avoid objects or situations that cause general distress, the therapist may recommend relaxation training, breathing retraining, and gradual reexposure to the school setting to help:

- reduce unpleasant physical symptoms,
- provide a way of coping with uncomfortable situations, and
- ease reentry into school.

If your child is refusing school to escape painful social and/or evaluative situations, the therapist may recommend role-play, practice in real-life situations, and cognitive therapy to help:

- build skills so that your child will master social situations,
- decrease social anxiety that interferes with performance, and
- reduce negative thinking that hampers school attendance.

If your child is refusing school for attention, the therapist may recommend parent training in contingency management to help:

- give you skills to improve your child's compliance to your commands,
- shift your attention to positive behaviors such as going to school, and
- put you more in charge of what is happening at home.

If your child is refusing school to pursue tangible rewards outside of school, the therapist may recommend contracting among family members to help:

- reduce family conflict by providing a method for problem-solving,
- increase rewards when your child attends school, and
- decrease rewards when your child misses school.

If your child is refusing school for two or more of these reasons, then two or more of these treatment plans will be needed. Other treatment components may be added as appropriate, and some are described in this workbook. Ask the therapist specific questions about his or her recommended treatment program. *Remember that you, as the client, can veto or change any treatment program that is suggested.*

Pretreatment Considerations

In addition to summarizing the assessment results and recommending a treatment plan, the therapist will talk about things that may affect treatment. Such things about your child might include:

- temperament/personality (e.g., hostility, sensitivity, motivation or reaction to change, introversion versus extroversion).

- degree of self-esteem, self-efficacy, and self-discipline (e.g., willingness to delay gratification, persistence in treatment).
- social status (e.g., popular, neglected, rejected) and degree of racial/ethnic dissonance from peers at school.
- verbal ability, intelligence, and academic status (e.g., high versus low grades).
- physical status (e.g., overweight, tall, athletic).
- other problems (e.g., hyperactivity, aggression, learning disability, running away from school).
- birth order and presence of siblings.
- presence of traumatic life events.
- attitude toward treatment and the therapist (e.g., willingness to talk).
- willingness to sabotage treatment procedures between sessions (e.g., refusing to complete homework assignments, becoming increasingly secretive about school refusal behavior over time).

Things about you or your family that may affect treatment might include:

- your methods of discipline and your relationship with your child.
- single- versus dual-parent family.
- conflict between you and your spouse or within the family.
- general family dynamics.
- parent anxiety, depression, or other problems.
- your family's financial and time resources.
- expectations and level of optimism versus pessimism regarding the treatment plan (including degree of commitment to the plan).
- your family's level of communication and problem-solving skill.
- cultural variables (e.g., different levels of acculturation, language differences, ethnic identity, mistrust of the therapist).

In addition, other things that may affect treatment might include:

- degree of cooperation from school officials and other school variables.
- persistence of school officials to convince you to implement a quicker treatment or treatment other than the one described in this workbook.
- cases referred by the family versus an external agency (e.g., court).
- restraints on the therapist's time and resources.
- school victimization.

The last item refers to children who feel they will be victimized in some way if they attend school. Many children, for example, are victims of theft, property damage, threat, and/or injury. Others are troubled by unpleasant teachers or unfair rules. In addition, the violence and shootings that sometimes take place in American schools concern many parents and children. Such incidents may induce or affect school refusal behavior in different ways. For example, a child may miss school because he or she is worried about genuine potential harm or a threatening situation there. In addition, a child may exaggerate claims of school victimization to manipulate parents into letting him or her stay home. Finally, a school's victimization rate may induce a parent to withdraw his or her child from school whether or not the child feels affected.

If any of these pretreatment considerations reveals pertinent information, the therapist may suggest a change in the treatment plan. For example, in cases where school officials are unwilling to help your child back into a classroom setting, then more responsibility for treatment may rest on you. It may be necessary to contact other people to help out with treatment if your time and resources are limited. In cases of potential school victimization, for example, the therapist may investigate whether a change of school is appropriate or if another intervention is warranted. Be flexible as different circumstances arise and remember that the therapist may change the treatment procedures at any time depending on your situation.

Scheduling Future Sessions

In addition to outlining the treatment plan, the therapist will describe how long treatment may last. This workbook assumes an average timeline of eight sessions in 4–8 weeks. However, your case may require less or more time. During treatment, talk with the therapist on a regular basis about the structure and scheduling of future sessions. Also, it is a good idea to talk to the therapist at this time about what to do in case you miss sessions or if other agencies (e.g., insurance company, your employer) limit the time you have available for therapy. Because the successful treatment of school refusal behavior is often an intense process, missing sessions can be disruptive. *It is therefore extremely important to make every effort to attend each therapy session and make-up missed sessions as soon as possible.*

Work Between Therapy Sessions

Much of the treatment success that you and your child achieve will come from the effort that you give between therapy sessions. Although the therapist can lay the groundwork for successful treatment, you and your child will have to do the hard work to make treatment pay off. Much of this hard work will come in the form of homework that the therapist will give to you and your child. Examples include completing logbooks, practicing treatment techniques, adhering to a regular school-day schedule, bringing your child to school, following through on instructions to change parenting behaviors, and adhering to written contracts developed in the sessions. Don't assume that the therapist is the cure-all for your situation. He or she can only accomplish what you and your child are willing to accomplish.

However, if you put forth sufficient effort, your chances for treatment success are very good. If you find during treatment that you or another family member cannot carry out a homework assignment, or if someone is deliberately sabotaging treatment, then discuss this with the therapist immediately.

General Procedures

Review of the Past Week and Feedback

At the beginning of each treatment session, the therapist will want to talk with you about events since the previous session. He or she will want to know of any changes in the family's situation or your child's school refusal behavior as well as anything else you deem important. Be sure to use this time to let the therapist know of any concerns or questions that you or your child have. The therapist will also want to see how you and your child carried out the homework assignments from the previous session. If there were problems, discuss them. Be sure to emphasize your child's successes as much as his or her difficulties.

In each treatment session, the therapist may also want to give you some feedback about your or your child's performance during the past few days. It is very important to listen carefully to the therapist and try and correct any problems. Remember, however, that you have a right to disagree with anything regarding the progress and structure of therapy. If you disagree, be open with the therapist and propose other remedies for current problems.

Discussion of Daily Logbooks

At the beginning of each treatment session, the therapist will also want to review the daily logbooks that you and your child are completing. The therapist will pay special attention to sudden changes in ratings, patterns in the ratings, differences between your ratings and your child's ratings, written comments, or missing ratings. *It is extremely important that you bring your and your child's completed logbooks to each session.* The therapist must have this information to track treatment progress and help you implement the best course of action regarding treatment. If you or your child are having any problems with the logbooks, be sure to discuss these problems with the therapist.

Procedures for Specific Treatment Sessions

Session 2

In each treatment program, the second treatment session is often very important because many of your child's school refusal behaviors will be dealt with directly. Therefore, your motivation and effort in therapy will be as important as ever. The therapist will continue to check your child's progress as indicated in your logbooks, and should have a good understanding of the trends in your child's behavior. Likewise, you should have a good relationship with the therapist at this point and feel comfortable asking questions. Remember, it is important that you and your child participate in, and follow through with, the treatment plan as much as possible.

Sessions 3–4

By sessions 3–4, the treatment process should be starting to mature as you become more comfortable with the therapist and the procedures that he or she is recommending. In addition, you should have a good idea where therapy is headed and what will be asked of you and/or your child. If you are uncertain, be sure to raise any questions with the therapist.

Sessions 3–4 often represent the "heavy lifting" portion of therapy. During these sessions, your child's school attendance will start, increase, or be tied more closely to rewards and punishments. As a result, you will spend more daily effort on the school refusal problem. Many family members have trouble with treatment at this stage because of the increased effort that is needed. Stick with the treatment program as long as possible and rely on the therapist for support and feedback. Often, the longer therapy continues, the greater the chances for success. In addition, continue to develop a close working relationship with school officials.

Sessions 5–6

By sessions 5–6, treatment should be quite intense and focused. Although different issues can be discussed at this time, you and the therapist should spend much of the time in session addressing your child's specific school refusal behaviors.

The procedures in sessions 5–6 should be used only if things are going fairly well up to now. If your child has started going to school or is going with more regularity, then the procedures discussed for sessions 5–6 may apply. However, if your child or family has so far seen less improvement, then the therapist may want to spend more time covering material from previous sessions. In many cases of school refusal behavior, "backtracking" to correct new or stubborn problems or relapses is not unusual. Remember that the procedures described in this workbook are meant to be flexible enough to fit your particular case. Some cases take more time and others take less time to resolve. Do not be too concerned if your therapy schedule does not exactly match the one described.

Sessions 7–8

By sessions 7–8, your child's school refusal behavior should be nearly resolved. As a result, these sessions may focus on tying up loose ends, completing full-time school attendance, branching out into other areas of concern, going over key themes from therapy, setting up long-term follow-up procedures, and/or preparing for the end of therapy. If treatment does extend longer than eight sessions, then you and the therapist may continue to rely on the principles and techniques described in this workbook. Extended treatment is often necessary for stubborn cases of school refusal behavior or in cases where other behavior problems need to be addressed.

Treatment success is sometimes defined as full-time school attendance for some period of time and/or a substantial reduction in the child's daily stress regarding school. However, each case is different and so you and the therapist may define treatment success differently. In some cases, for example, full-time school attendance for several weeks or a complete lack of child anxiety regarding school is needed to define treatment success. In other cases, especially those of adolescents with chronic absenteeism, even part-time school attendance is a good definition of success. Whatever your definition of success, do not leave therapy until you have had a thorough discussion of all relevant issues with the therapist.

Stepping Down the Therapy Program

The latter sessions of therapy may be spaced apart to give you and your child time to test new skills and uncover less obvious anxieties and worries about school. Homework assignments may be given as appropriate and will likely mirror those given in earlier sessions. Sessions may be scheduled every other week or monthly through the end of the school year. This tapering of treatment sessions will give you and your child a sense of support and convey the message that your child is doing well and can handle any anxious situations. In addition, this tapering of treatment sessions will allow you and/or your family to refine the treatment procedures discussed in this workbook.

The final steps of treatment will be ensured as your and your child's self-confidence improve and you and your child gain more experience handling a wide range of situations. Although the therapist will work with you and your child to eventually terminate treatment, it is important for both of you to end therapy systematically, say goodbye to the therapist, and discuss plans for the future.

The End of Treatment

When should treatment end? Ultimately, this is a question best answered following a thorough discussion with the therapist. Some parents and children prefer to end treatment as soon as the child is back in school, but this approach is discouraged. In many cases, residual problems and questions remain, or the child "tests" his or her parents by refusing school one day a couple of weeks later. An appropriate analogy to consider is what happens when you are prescribed an antibiotic medication. This medicine usually must be taken for ten full days, long after the symptoms dissipate. If you stop the medication once the symptoms disappear, you may place yourself at risk of relapse due to an incomplete course of treatment. Similarly, the therapist, you, and your child need to fully wrap up work together before it ends. This may involve tapered sessions and relapse prevention training. Chapter 8 describes specific techniques used by therapists to ensure that children stay on course and avoid slips or relapse.

In other cases, families have problems that go beyond the child's school refusal behavior. Treatments regarding these other problems should therefore continue even if the child is back in school. Common examples of such problems include general family conflict, anxiety, depression, lack of motivation, delinquent and oppositional behavior, learning disability, and hyperactivity, among others. In complex cases such as these, extended treatment is often appropriate and desirable to make sure the child stays in school and to address these other problems.

Reading This Workbook

Chapters 4–7 in this workbook discuss the different treatments for school refusal behavior. If your child is refusing school only to avoid objects or situations that cause general distress, then proceed to Chapter 4. If your child is refusing school only to escape painful social and/or evaluative situations, then proceed to Chapter 5. If your child is refusing school only for attention, then proceed to Chapter 6. If your child is refusing school only to pursue tangible rewards outside of school, then proceed to Chapter 7. If your child is refusing school for multiple reasons, then proceed to those treatment chapters that are most relevant.

Note that some material in this workbook may apply to different reasons why children refuse school. Examples include the sections on escorting a child to school and downplaying excessive reassurance-seeking. Therefore, you should read each section in this workbook in case it is necessary and in case you find a particular point relevant to your situation. *However, it is essential that you discuss any new treatment technique with the therapist before trying it on your own.*

Children Refusing School to Avoid Objects or Situations That Cause General Distress

Session 1: Starting Treatment

School refusal behavior is often motivated by a desire to avoid emotions such as dread, anxiety, panic, or depression that can become associated with certain school-related objects or situations. For children who avoid objects or situations provoking such general distress, the main goal of treatment is to change the child's avoidance behavior and build coping and active school attendance behaviors. Treatment for this condition will involve:

- building an anxiety and avoidance hierarchy of objects and situations,
- teaching somatic management skills to decrease negative emotional arousal,
- conducting systematic exposure to anxiety cues identified on a hierarchy in a step-by-step fashion, and
- accessing self-reinforcement for coping with transient negative emotions.

Treatment thus involves training your child to use self-control procedures. During this treatment program, your child will learn to identify personally relevant objects and situations that provoke anxiety, and use specific somatic skills to prevent himself or herself from experiencing a full-blown anxiety reaction. Gradually, your child will enter those situations that are most anxiety-provoking while using these somatic management skills.

The therapist will spend the majority of each session with your child, but will invite you to the last part of each session to give your input, review the material covered in that session, and plan homework. The therapist may enlist your assistance with your child's homework assignments, and it will be helpful if you set aside uninterrupted time for these practices and make them a family activity.

Psychoeducation

The therapist will begin treatment by helping your child understand the nature and process of anxiety. As your child's understanding of anxiety progresses, the therapist will help your child observe his or her own anxiety reactions, identify where anxiety reactions occur, and use specific skills or tools to cope with negative emotions. The following is an example of how the therapist might explain the process of anxiety to your child:

> When you're scared (anxious, upset), it feels like there's one big ball of bad stuff rolling over you, and there's nothing you can do to stop it. It's like a train is going to run you over! If you feel scared in that way, then you stay upset, and feel like you can't handle the situation. But, being scared (anxious, upset) is really made up of three parts. First is what you feel. All those feelings in your body that let you know you're scared. Things like your heart beating fast, shaking, your hands feeling sweaty, and butterflies in your stomach are all signals that you're scared. The

second part to being scared is what you say to yourself. Usually, you say something like *Get me out of here, I'm afraid, I can't do this, I want to go home*, or *I need Mom or someone to help me*. And finally, the third part to being scared is what you do when you're scared. This is usually something like leaving a place, or avoiding going to a place, or trying to be near someone who can help you feel better.

The therapist will ask your child to provide personally relevant responses to each of the three components of anxiety: physical (*What I feel*), cognitive (*What I think*), and behavioral (*What I do*). The therapist may draw three circles, each depicting a component of anxiety, and ask your child to identify his or her own physical feelings, thoughts, and behaviors when confronting an anxiety-provoking school situation. The therapist may use cartoons or pictures from magazines depicting children in school situations, and ask your child to describe what the child in the picture may be feeling, thinking, and doing. In this way, the therapist and your child can build rapport, understand what provokes anxiety, and understand how your child interprets various situations. The therapist can illustrate to your child the process of escalating anxiety, and the opposite process of calming or de-escalation.

In this way, the therapist can identify targets for change within each component. The therapist will then describe to your child the way in which these three components interact, each adding to the other to spiral into overwhelming feelings of anxiety. The therapist will emphasize the physical sensations of anxiety, how these sensations spiral to uncomfortable levels, and the resulting avoidance behavior that occurs. The therapist will explain that your child will learn to use specific skills to address each component. Your child will learn to use relaxation and deep breathing to manage his or her physical feelings of anxiety; step-by-step practices of entering anxious situations to change avoidance and escape behaviors; self-reinforcement and pride and praise to change the negative thoughts that accompany his or her anxiety.

Building an Anxiety and Avoidance Hierarchy

Using information gathered from the assessment interviews and logbooks, the therapist will help your child build his or her Anxiety and Avoidance Hierarchy (AAH; see Figure A.5). This is a list of the objects and situations that the therapist and your child will target for change over the course of treatment. Using a Feelings Thermometer (see Figure A.6) or other measurement scale, your child will rate his or her anxiety and avoidance of these objects and situations at each session. The therapist may also ask for your input when building the AAH.

Figure 4.1 shows a sample AAH of a 7-year-old girl who refused to attend school due to separation anxiety concerns. As you can see, the steps on Sandy's AAH are gradual so that she can begin with the easiest (or lowest) item and then progress up to the most difficult (highest) hierarchy item. This is how your child's treatment will proceed.

Anxiety and Avoidance Hierarchy

Problem: *School refusal due to anxiety about being away from home and from her parents*

Situations or Places That Scare Me!	Anxiety Rating	Avoidance Rating
1. *Staying in school all day without calling Mom and Dad*	8	8
2. *Staying in school all morning, and not calling Mom or Dad, or going to the nurse*	8	8
3. *Riding the school bus all by myself*	7	8
4. *Waiting for Mom, and she's late to pick me up*	6	7
5. *Staying with the babysitter, and Mom doesn't call home to check on us*	5	5
6. *Getting my school clothes ready the night before school*	5	3
7. *Having tutoring at the school, without Mom there*	4	2
8. *Going to school to get my homework, and visiting with my teacher*	3	2
9. *Going to lunch at school*	3	2
10. *Meeting with the tutor while Mom goes shopping*	3	2

Figure 4.1. **Sandy's Anxiety and Avoidance Hierarchy**

Relaxation Training and Breathing Retraining Exercises

The therapist will next begin to teach your child methods of relaxation and deep breathing. Ideally, the therapist will audiotape this segment for your child to use at home. If a tape recorder is not available, use the Relaxation and Deep Breathing Scripts. Your child will be asked to find a comfortable position in a chair or couch and to either close his or her eyes or let his or her gaze settle and focus on one spot in the room. The therapist will then talk your child through a series of muscle tension and relaxation exercises. These exercises are designed to teach your child to discriminate between the physical sensations of tension and calmness. The therapist will focus your child on "letting go" of tension and feeling calm and relaxed. It will be important for your child to isolate each muscle group one at a time, and so the therapist will direct your child to tense only a particular muscle (this step can be difficult for younger children). The therapist will emphasize deep breathing (into the stomach or diaphragm) as a way to prolong the relaxation and make it more complete. The therapist will use imagery to help younger children follow these exercises. The entire process of relaxation takes about 20 minutes. Following this process, the therapist may call you in for a discussion and summary of this first session.

Relaxation and Deep Breathing Scripts

Relaxation script (modified from Ollendick & Cerny, 1981)

Have your child recline in a comfortable position and either close his or her eyes or focus on one spot on the wall or ceiling. Your child's leg and arms should not be crossed. Have your child take off shoes and loosen any tight clothing (e.g., belts). Allow your child time to perform the muscle tension and relaxation exercises as described. Tensed muscles are to be held in place for approximately five seconds.

> I would like you to sit as comfortably as possible in your chair. During the next few minutes, I am going to give you some instructions about tensing and releasing different muscle groups. I want you to listen carefully and do what I ask you to do. Be sure not to anticipate what I say—just relax and concentrate on my voice. Any questions? (Answer questions as they occur.) Okay, put your feet on the floor, and put your arms on the arms of the chair. (Child focuses or closes eyes as desired.) Try to relax as much as possible.

Hands and arms

> Make a fist with your left hand. Squeeze it hard. Feel the tightness in your hand and arm as you squeeze. Now let your hand go and relax. See how much better your hand and arm feel when they are relaxed. Once again, make a fist with your left hand and squeeze hard. Good. Now relax and let your hand go. (Repeat the process for the right hand and arm.)

Arms and shoulders

Stretch your arms out in front of you. Raise them up high over your head. Way back. Feel the pull in your shoulders. Stretch higher. Now just let your arms drop back to your side. Okay, let's stretch again. Stretch your arms out in front of you. Raise them over your head. Pull them back, way back. Pull hard. Now let them drop quickly. Good. Notice how your shoulders feel more relaxed. This time let's have a great big stretch. Try to touch the ceiling. Stretch your arms out in front of you. Raise them way up over your head. Push them way, way back. Notice the tension and pull in your arms and shoulders. Hold tight, now. Great. Let them drop very quickly and feel how good it is to be relaxed. It feels good and warm and lazy.

Shoulders and neck

Try to pull your shoulders up to your ears and push your head down into your shoulders. Hold in tight. Okay, now relax and feel the warmth. Again, pull your shoulders up to your ears and push your head down into your shoulders. Do it tightly. Okay, you can relax now. Bring your head out and let your shoulders relax. Notice how much better it feels to be relaxed than to be all tight. One more time now. Push your head down and your shoulders way up to your ears. Hold it. Feel the tenseness in your neck and shoulders. Okay. You can relax now and feel comfortable. You feel good.

Jaw

Put your teeth together real hard. Let your neck muscles help you. Now relax. Just let your jaw hang loose. Notice how good it feels just to let your jaw drop. Okay, bite down hard. That's good. Now relax again. Just let your jaw drop. It feels so good just to let go. Okay, one more time. Bite down. Hard as you can. Harder. Oh, you really are working hard. Good. Now relax. Try to relax your whole body. Let yourself get as loose as you can.

Face and nose

Wrinkle up your nose. Make as many wrinkles in your nose as you can. Scrunch up your nose real hard. Good. Now relax your nose. Now wrinkle up your nose again. Wrinkle it up hard. Hold it just as tight as you can. Okay. You can relax your face. Notice that when you scrunch up your nose your cheeks and your mouth and your forehead all help you and they get tight, too. So when you relax your nose, your whole face relaxes too, and that feels good. Now make lots of wrinkles on your forehead. Hold it tight, now. Okay, you can let go. Now you can just relax. Let your face go smooth. No wrinkles anywhere. Your face feels nice and smooth and relaxed.

Stomach

Now tighten up your stomach muscles real tight. Make your stomach real hard. Don't move. Hold it. You can relax now. Let your stomach go soft. Let it be as relaxed as you can. That feels so much better. Okay, again. Tighten your stomach real hard. Good. You can relax now. Settle down, get comfortable and relax. Notice the difference between a tight stomach and a relaxed one. That's how we want to feel. Nice and loose and relaxed. Okay. Once more. Tighten up. Tighten hard. Good. Now you can relax completely. You feel nice and relaxed.

This time, try to pull your stomach in. Try to squeeze it against your backbone. Try to be as skinny as you can. Now relax. You don't have to be skinny now. Just relax and feel your stomach being warm and loose. Okay, squeeze in your stomach again. Make it touch your backbone. Get it real small and tight. Get as skinny as you can. Hold tight now. You can relax now. Settle back and let your stomach come back out where it belongs. You can feel really good now. You've done fine.

Legs and feet

Push your toes down on the floor real hard. You'll probably need your legs to help you push. Push down, spread your toes apart. Now relax your feet. Let your toes go loose and feel how nice that is. It feels good to be relaxed. Okay. Now push your toes down. Let your leg muscles help you put your feet down. Push your feet. Hard. Okay. Relax your feet, relax your legs, relax your toes. It feels so good to be relaxed. No tenseness anywhere. You kind of feel warm and tingly.

Conclusion

Stay as relaxed as you can. Let your whole body go limp and feel all your muscles relaxed. In a few minutes it will be the end of the relaxation exercise. Today is a good day. You've worked hard in here and it feels good to work hard. Okay, shake your arms. Now shake your legs. Move your head around. Open your eyes slowly. Very good. You've done a good job. You're going to be a super relaxer.

Breathing retraining script

Ask your child to imagine going on a hot air balloon ride. Tell your child that as long as the hot air balloon has fuel supplied by your child's breathing, destinations are unlimited. Ask your child to breathe in through his or her nose and out through his or her mouth with a SSSSSSSSS sound. You may encourage this process by having a picture of a hot air balloon nearby. If necessary, have your child count to himself or herself slowly when breathing out. The following is an example.

Imagine going on a ride in a hot air balloon. Your breathing will give the balloon its power. As long as you breathe deeply, the balloon can go anywhere. Breathe in through your nose like this (parent demonstrates). Breathe slowly and deeply. Try to breathe in a lot of air. Now breathe out slowly through your mouth, making a hissing sound like this (parent demonstrates). If you want, you can count to yourself when you breathe in and out.

Homework

Homework assignments after session 1 may include the following:

- Practice the relaxation and breathing procedure at home every day, twice a day if possible, between sessions. Record each practice on the relaxation log provided in Figure 4.2. Note any particular difficulties encountered during the practice (e.g., inability to concentrate, falling asleep during practice).
- Continue to complete the daily logbooks, noting any specific issues or situations that arise during the week.

Session 2: Intensifying Treatment

In this session, the therapist will begin to present to your child those objects or situations that provoke his or her anxiety. This process will occur through a procedure called systematic desensitization. First through imagination (*imaginal* exposure), then using real-life situations (*in vivo* exposure), your child will confront his or her anxieties in a step-by-step fashion. Between sessions, your child will practice imaginal and real-life exposures, or "Show That I Can" (STIC) tasks (Kendall et al., 1992). STIC tasks reinforce and extend the treatment techniques introduced during the session. The therapist will enlist your help in setting up and conducting these STIC tasks.

Preparing Your Child for the Systematic Desensitization Process

The term systematic desensitization will be explained to your child if he or she is an older adolescent and can understand more complex concepts. Otherwise, the therapist will provide your child with an explanation such as in the following dialogue. In the dialogue, **T** represents the therapist, and **C** represents the child.

T: Let me ask you something. Do you know how to ride a bike? Or swim? Or do you ski or ride horses? (The therapist will ask until he or she finds some activity that your child is able to perform with some skill.)

Relaxation Practice Log

Name: ______________________________

Day	Practice 1		Practice 2	
	Time	How did you feel?	Time	How did you feel?

Figure 4.2.

C: Yes, I can ride a bicycle. I learned that when I was five or six.

T: Okay, tell me about what you do when you want to go biking (skiing, horseback riding).

C: Well, I get my bike out of the garage, and I ride it up the street or to my friend's house.

T: Okay, you have to get the bike out of the garage. What do you think about when you're riding your bike?

C: Nothing. I mean, I think about what me and my friend are going to do. Like maybe we'll play video games.

T: Are you riding your bike in the street or on the sidewalk?

C: Well, I have to ride on the sidewalk. But sometimes I have to cross the street, so I look both ways.

T: And what are you doing with your hands, and feet, and your eyes when you ride?

C: Nothing. I just pedal, and hold the handlebars. And I have to look where I'm going.

T: Okay. So, what you're telling me is that you get on the bike, ride along the sidewalks and street, pedal along, and watch where you're going, and you don't think about those things. Instead, you think about what you're going to do with your friend. Right?

C: Yeah, I guess.

T: Sure, it's automatic that you ride now, and watch out for where you're going. You've learned how to do these things, haven't you? (Child nods.) And you don't even think about how you're doing these things anymore. But, do you remember when you first went out on the bike? Do you remember that it first used to be scary?

The therapist will question your child and prompt him or her to recall the first time riding a bike or doing some similar activity that requires skill. The therapist will ask your child to identify the physical feelings, thoughts, and behaviors of a child who is learning to ride for the first time. The therapist will then ask your child about his or her initial learning experiences—how initial steps were small, but with practice your child developed skill and mastery. At this point, the therapist will focus your child on how continued practice and overlearning has made the situation easy and automatic. The therapist will ask your child about what happened to his or her initial anxieties.

T: Why aren't you scared of falling off the bike now?

C: Because I don't fall anymore. And if I do, I may get scraped, but it gets better.

T: So, even if you do fall, you know that you're going to be okay. Right?

C: Yeah, I've fallen. I just have to get on the bike again. That way I don't get scared again.

T: Right! That's exactly right! You have practiced riding your bike, and you started out in steps. Someone helped you, and you used training wheels. Then you took them off when you started feeling more comfortable and less afraid. Right? So you did this step-by-step and, as you developed more skill, you became less afraid. Now you don't even think about how you were once afraid.

The therapist will then introduce your child to the concept of taking steps one at a time and mastering each step until very little or no anxiety is felt. This will be accomplished through the imaginal desensitization process, which the therapist may present to your child as "practicing thinking about the troubling situations." During the imaginal desensitization process, the therapist will describe anxiety-provoking scenes from your child's AAH, and alternate them with relaxing scenes.

Constructing the Anxiety Scenario

The therapist will choose one of the easier steps from your child's AAH. This will be the first situation to confront imaginally. The therapist will ask your child about what he or she thinks will happen in the situation, and develop a scenario about that situation based on what your child thinks and is anxious about. The therapist may embellish the scenario to some degree. Often, parents are surprised at the graphic nature and intensity of their child's anxieties. However, it is important to note that these are your child's anxieties and, left to his or her imagination, they can continue to develop unchecked. The therapist will help your child think about these anxieties, mix in relaxing scenes so the thoughts themselves are no longer frightening, and then discuss what is realistic for any given situation. The goal of imaginal desensitization is to gradually get your child to listen to an entire anxiety scenario "as if watching a movie" and realize that the scenario is not that frightening in itself. Another goal is to have your child recognize that he or she can cope with just about any scenario in a positive, proactive way. The following is a sample scenario using situation 8 from Sandy's AAH (see Figure 4.1):

> It's after two o'clock, and you and your mother are driving to school to see your teacher. You have to go in and get your own homework. You haven't been in school for three weeks, and haven't really seen any of the other kids or the teacher. The last time you were there you felt real funny in your stomach, and you felt like throwing up. As you get closer to school, you start to feel a bit dizzy, and start to sweat a bit. You look up at Mom, and want her to turn the car around, but she says you have to get the work. Mom has to stay in the car, because there's no place to park, so you have to go in alone. Mom drives up to the front door of the school. Some kids are there, and some teachers, but not yours or anyone you know. You open the car door, and feel really dizzy now, and your stomach feels like you're on a roller coaster. You start to walk up to the door, and you feel really shaky and you're sweating. These are the feelings that you get sometimes that scare you. What if you get sick? You look back, and Mom is moving the car and is now pulling out of the school driveway. You walk in through the door, and feel so dizzy that you have to hold on to the wall to stay standing. Some kids walk by and laugh. You're really feeling scared now, and it's getting harder to breathe. What if you faint, and no one comes to get you and help you? What if Mom just stays in the car? You start walking down the long hall to the classroom, and when you get there, several kids are in line to see the teacher. So, you have to wait. It's really hot in the classroom, and you feel like you can throw up again. You're so dizzy now, and can taste real sour stuff coming up in your throat. You feel dizzy and faint, and wish that the teacher would look at you and help you, but she's talking to someone else. You can feel it coming now, it's at the top of your throat. You yell out for help, and when you do, you get sick all over the place. The teacher and all the kids are looking at you now, with wide eyes. You feel really sick, and really embarrassed. If only your mother had come in with you.

Tracking Anxiety During Desensitization

Throughout the systematic desensitization process, the therapist will ask your child to rate his or her anxiety levels using the Feelings Thermometer or other measurement scale. The therapist will record your child's ratings. This way, the therapist can illustrate, using charts or graphs, what happened to your child's anxiety during the systematic desensitization. These charts or graphs will show how your child gradually mastered his or her anxiety over the course of treatment.

Some children are able to track their own anxiety levels. Recording his or her own ratings gives a child instant information about how he or she handled certain situations. The ratings can illustrate how the child coped with panic symptoms, separation concerns, anxiety about specific objects or situations, or any other situation where anxiety ratings can be taken and recorded. You may wish to keep your child's ratings in a log or notebook to remind your child of progress made during therapy.

Conducting the Imaginal Desensitization

The therapist will likely audiotape the imaginal desensitization procedure for later processing and for home use as a STIC task. The desensitization begins with the therapist instructing your child to raise his or her hand whenever anxiety makes him or her uncomfortable. This is indicated by a level of 3 or above on the Feelings Thermometer. The therapist will explain that he or she will first have your child relax, and will then begin presenting the troubling scene. Your child is to listen to the therapist and imagine the scene in his or her mind as if it is actually happening. When anxiety becomes uncomfortable, he or she should raise a hand. At that point, the therapist will ask your child to switch to thinking about something pleasant, such as being on a beach, in the park, or in some other place that is relaxing and pleasing for your child. Once the anxiety falls back to a level of 0 or 1, the therapist will again begin to present the troubling scene. This switching back and forth will continue until your child is able to tolerate listening to the scene all the way through without uncomfortable levels of anxiety.

As your child begins to progress through each scene, the therapist will ask him or her to raise a hand when anxiety reaches a level of 4 or 5. This allows your child to develop increased tolerance and eventually habituate to the sensations and feelings of anxiety. As tolerance increases, these feelings will lose their ability to signal your child to escape or avoid, and will allow him or her to try new situations while tolerating normal levels of arousal. If necessary, the therapist will divide the anxiety scenario into smaller steps or less volatile scenes. The imaginal desensitization process always ends with a relaxation scene.

Processing the Imaginal Desensitization

Once the imaginal desensitization is completed, the therapist may call you in to the session to discuss your child's progress. The therapist may play some of the tape for you and ask your child to explain and demonstrate the process to you. The therapist will then question your child: "What happened to your anxiety while we did this practice?" The therapist may illustrate the habituation of anxiety by drawing graphs or diagrams of your child's anxiety ratings throughout the desensitization process. This will show how the anxiety dissipated with each succeeding presentation. For example, compare Sandy's anxiety about riding the school bus in her first imaginal desensitization session with her anxiety in a later in vivo, or real-life, desensitization practice (Figure 4.3).

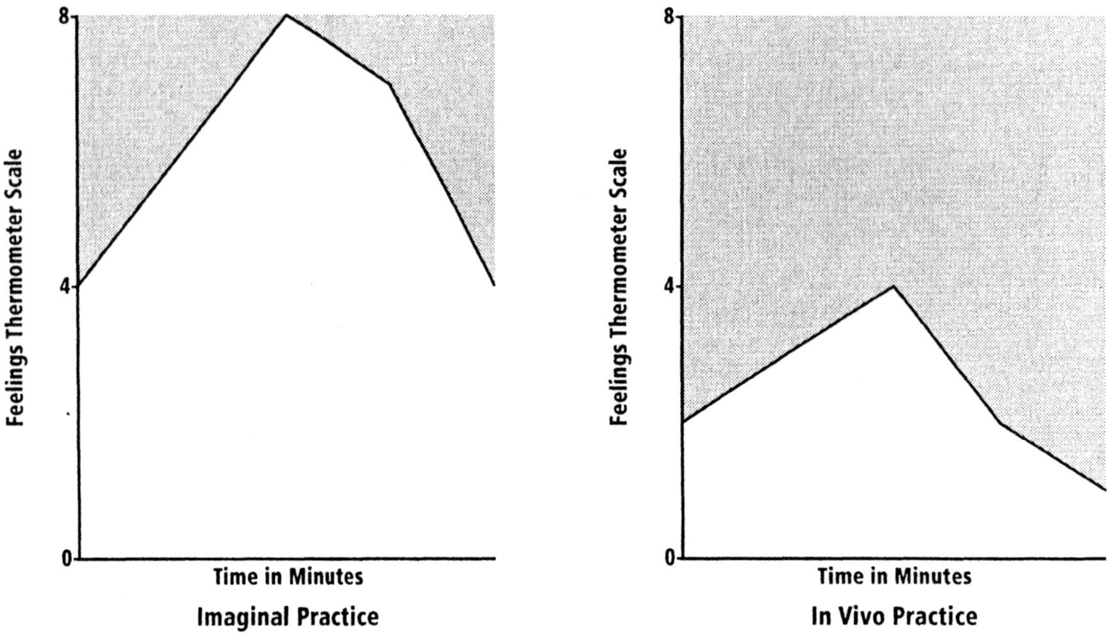

Figure 4.3. Sandy's Anxiety Ratings

Using the first graph, the therapist can show Sandy how she was initially very anxious about riding the bus, given that her anxiety ratings began near 3 and very quickly reached their worst level of 8. Furthermore, the therapist can emphasize that this simply involved Sandy's imagination. On the second graph, Sandy can clearly see that, during a real-life (in vivo) ride on the school bus, her anxiety started on a lower level, peaked at a lower level, and went away much faster than before. Sandy therefore learned that what she imagines is often worse than what will actually occur, and that she can handle the situation despite her anxiety.

Even if your child did not habituate (i.e., ratings did not go down), the therapist will praise your child for any effort or degree of participation and process what may have been particularly difficult for your child. In such cases, which are not unusual, the anxiety scenario can be broken down into smaller steps or less volatile scenes. It is important that your child be given praise and encouragement for making any step, no matter how small. Typically, desensitization begins slowly, and the pace quickens over time. This may occur in one session or across two or more sessions if necessary.

If your child did not readily habituate, the therapist may process with your child what thoughts he or she may be having during the exposure. For particularly troublesome or negative thoughts, the therapist may use cognitive restructuring procedures (see Chapter 5). These procedures will enhance your child's ability to identify and change negative thoughts.

Homework

Homework assignments after session 2 may require more assistance on your part and may include the following:

- Continue to practice the relaxation procedure using the relaxation tape just before bedtime each night.
- At least once daily, your child should listen to the desensitization tape and go through an imaginal desensitization practice (STIC task). You may assist your child by asking for anxiety ratings, or by keeping other children who are at home from interrupting the procedure. You should talk with your child after each practice, much like the therapist did during the session. Focus your child on how his or her anxiety dissipated and offer praise and encouragement for attempting and/or completing each practice.
- Wake your child about 90–120 minutes before school is scheduled to start and implement the normal school-day routine. Follow this routine as closely as possible. During the day, your child should do schoolwork and read school-related books when at home.
- Continue to complete the daily logbooks, noting any specific issues or situations that arise during the week.

Sessions 3–4: Maturing of Treatment

Sessions 3–4 will continue to focus on systematic desensitization, with an introduction to in vivo desensitization. In vivo desensitization involves having your child gradually enter the anxiety-producing situation and use his or her relaxation techniques to manage anxiety. Your help will be crucial to the success of this process, as you will be expected to arrange the time and place of the in vivo desensitization and help your child engage the situation.

Continuing the Systematic Desensitization

The therapist will review your child's progress in listening to the imaginal desensitization tape (STIC task) and discuss any problems encountered during the week. If your child did not comply with the STIC task, the therapist will address the reasons why this occurred. Some children avoid doing the homework to avoid any rising feelings of anxiety. It may be that the anxiety scenario needs to be divided into smaller steps, or the therapist may program "coping scenes" during the desensitization. If your child is having a particularly difficult time listening to the scene, and is unable to habituate to the anxiety, then the therapist can present images of your child and a favorite superhero or athlete confronting and coping with the situation. For example:

You are waiting for your mother to pick you up after school, but she is late! As you stand out front, the other kids are all being picked up, and the teachers have gone back into the school or driven home. It's really getting late, and you are worried that something may have happened to Mom. What if something bad happens to you? You notice that the sky is getting dark, and big thunderclouds are coming. It starts to thunder, and flashes of lightning are happening. You try to go back into the school, but now the door is locked! Where is Mom? You are really scared now, and feel like crying. You think something terrible must have happened to Mom, and now you could get caught in the lightning! But wait! You start to think, "What would Michael Jordan do in this situation?" There must have been times when he had to wait for his parents, and probably he was alone and outside too. Would he cry if he were here? What would he tell you to do? Picture Michael Jordan standing next to you. He says, "Okay, you're afraid that something bad happened to Mom, but why else could she be late?" You answer, "Well, Michael, maybe she's in traffic, and there's a lot of cars; or maybe she had to run an errand and it's taking a bit longer than she thought." Michael tells you, "Yeah! Good thought! She could just be running late. Now, what should you do about the weather here?" Now picture yourself telling Michael, "Well, I suppose I could stand under the awning, and wait by the door. That way I can see Mom when she comes, and I'll be out of the storm." "Great job," says Michael. "Take some deep breaths, and wait by the door for her. She'll be here soon." Michael gives you a high-five, and you feel so proud! Now, picture yourself going to the door, standing under the awning, and waiting calmly for Mom.

Some children avoid their STIC tasks because they anticipate that getting better means getting back into school more quickly. If this is happening with your child, the therapist will focus your child on the goals of the program and examine whether additional factors (e.g., attention-seeking, tangible rewards for staying home) need to be addressed more directly in treatment.

The therapist will continue to develop scenarios for each item on your child's AAH, and progress to more challenging items sequentially. Thus, progress will be evident when your child listens to an entire AAH scenario, does not have to switch to a neutral, relaxing scene, and reports minimal anxiety ratings.

Introducing Your Child to the In Vivo Desensitization

In vivo desensitization involves entering and confronting real-life situations or activities. For this part of treatment, the therapist must help your child make a link between imaginal confrontation of anxiety-provoking situations and actually entering these situations. For example:

T: Okay, let's think about something. Remember when we talked about how you learned to ride a bicycle?

C: Yes, from practice.

T: Right. And you've been doing a great job in here, practicing here and at home imagining doing these things that make you upset.

C: Yes, I "Show That I Can" all the time. I do my practice every day!

T: Yep. That's great! Let's think about something. Suppose that you didn't know how to ride a bicycle. Suppose it was back to that time before you learned how to do that. Can you remember that?

C: Yes, I remember.

T: Okay. Now, suppose that I show you a movie about how to ride a bicycle. And you watch the movie again and again. But, you just watch the movie, you never really get to try a bicycle. Do you think it would be easy to just get on a bike and ride?

C: No, I have to practice on a bike. I'd be all wobbly and could fall down if I don't practice.

T: Right! So, watching the movie may help you to know what it looks like to ride. And, it may show you some things to think about while you ride. But, you really have to try a bicycle again and again, to practice and learn how to ride.

C: That's right. You have to get on the bicycle to learn how to ride it.

T: Well, the same thing goes here. We've been imagining going into these situations that scare you, and you've been doing a great job of learning that you don't have to be scared. But, we need to help you really go into these situations and practice really being there. Do you understand what I mean?

C: So, I have to ride the school bus?

T: Well, eventually, yes. But first, we'll only practice for real the situations we've done in here and on tape. And we'll work up to the bus and those other things that are really scary for you. We'll do this step-by-step, just like we do in your imagination. We'll first do it in your imagination, and then we'll do it for real. Taking it easy, going one step at a time, and we'll get Mom and Dad to help out here and there.

Conducting the First In Vivo Desensitization

The therapist will role-play with your child one of the easier items from your child's AAH. These role-play trials, made as close to reality as possible, will involve your child acting out and confronting an anxiety-provoking situation. For example, if your child is anxious about being alone either at school or home, the therapist will construct a situation where your child waits in a therapy room by himself or herself for a period of time. Initially, the situation will be set up to be minimally anxiety-provoking and your child will be encouraged to use the relaxation and deep breathing skills to manage anxiety. As your child develops tolerance of the situation, the therapist will slowly make these situations more challenging and encourage your child to refrain from using any safety behaviors to make himself or herself feel better. Below are examples of trials in a graduated in vivo desensitization for a child who is afraid to be left waiting alone:

1. Sitting alone in the therapy room for 3 and then 5 minutes, knowing that the therapist is in the hall.
2. Sitting alone in the therapy room for 5 and then 10 minutes, knowing that the therapist may not be in the hall.
3. Sitting alone in the therapy room for 10 minutes, with the lights dimmed, knowing that the therapist is not in the hall.
4. Sitting alone in the therapy room, not knowing how long it will be, with the lights dimmed, the therapist not in the hall, and Mom or Dad told to not be in the waiting room.

Desensitization trials begin with assistance from the therapist and with relatively easier situations. The demands will increase with each successive trial. Your child's expectations are also addressed, as he or she initially knows what to expect in the situation (e.g., trial 1, knowing the therapist is in the hall), but is later exposed to unknowns (e.g., trial 4, *not* knowing how long it will be). This process is designed to build up your child's ability to cope with ambiguous, challenging, and often uncontrollable situations. Anxiety often results from feeling unable to control or predict what could happen in any situation, and from concern that something very negative will occur. These desensitization trials teach your child that, even when he or she does not have total control of a situation, he or she can still cope effectively and that the worst scenario is not likely to occur. Your child learns to tolerate normal levels of anxiety while gathering information about his or her coping resources and skills.

The therapist will invite you in to review progress with your child. Your child will tell you about the in vivo desensitization, and the therapist will review with you how the daily routine has been progressing. There will be specific instructions on what steps to take next in getting your child more used to, and involved with, the school routine. For example, the next STIC task may involve a trip to the school library or meeting after school hours with the teacher to pick up homework. These tasks combine the in vivo desensitization process with the STIC tasks. The therapist will discuss any potential problems with adherence to the school schedule, and make recommendations as needed.

Setting the Pace of, and Assistance With, the In Vivo Exposures

There are several ways to set the pace of in vivo exposures. A slower pace is preferred for younger children, those with special needs, and those with exceptionally high levels of anxiety. This allows the child to fully habituate to the anxiety, overlearn the plan of confronting the stressor, and build trust that he or she will not be forced into anything overwhelming.

During *assisted in vivo exposure,* either you or the therapist performs the exposure with your child. This allows your child to receive support from a trusted individual and observe a model who manages the situation. A careful balance must be struck between *modeling,* where you show the child how to manage the situation, and *rescuing,* where you take over and do the situation for your child. Assisted in vivo exposure keeps the focus on your child, with the goal of having him or her confront the stressor and manage the situation himself or herself. Typically, the therapist first models for your child how to deal with the situation while your child observes. Next, the therapist helps your child manage the situation. Your child and the therapist (or parent) then engage in the situation as a team. Next, your child manages the situation on his or her own, with words of encouragement from the team. Finally, your child engages the situation on his or her own while verbalizing self-reinforcement for performing the in vivo desensitization.

In *massed exposure* or *flooding,* your child confronts a stressor at a high intensity. Rather than gradually progressing up the AAH, the therapist chooses a higher item and begins there. Relaxation procedures are typically downplayed, so the advantage of flooding is that it takes less time. Your child simply enters the anxiety-producing situation and stays with it until anxiety naturally dissipates. Flooding is not often used with young children, when anxiety is extreme, at the beginning of therapy, for children with chronic school refusal behavior, or for children with social and/or evaluative anxieties. Deciding to use more rapid flooding procedures depends on your child's progress to this point and whether he or she understands the reason for this process.

Homework

Homework assignments after sessions 3–4 may include the following:

- Continue to practice the relaxation tape at bedtime.
- Listen to and conduct a tape (imaginal) desensitization procedure. Do this at least once daily.
- Practice an additional STIC task that involves a minimum of 3 different days of in vivo desensitization practice. This task will be agreed upon by the therapist, your child, and yourself. The in vivo desensitization may involve any of the following: practice at home, such as practicing staying alone in a room or in the house for varying periods of time; allowing you to leave the house and staying with a sitter for varying periods or time; visiting the school bus stop in the morning; visiting the school or some room at the school; or similar situations. You will have to agree to make the time to assist your child with these in vivo practices. The therapist will give you and your child specific instructions for conducting the practice.
- Continue to follow a regular school-day schedule, with early wakening, typical dressing and preparing for school, and completing school assignments. Avoid inadvertently reinforcing your child for not going to school. For example, it may be easier for you to take your child to the store or on errands; however, these types of outings serve to reinforce your child's avoidance of school, increase dependence on you, and give a message that it is acceptable to be home. Arranging for a sitter or, in the case of responsible older children, leaving your child alone for specified periods, is preferred to taking him or her with you on such excursions.
- Continue to complete the daily logbooks, noting any specific issues or situations that arise during the week.

Sessions 5–6: Advanced Maturing of Treatment

Sessions 5–6 involve helping your child move more swiftly and aggressively through the AAH. Thus, it is imperative that you and your child make every effort to arrange and complete the assigned in vivo desensitization practices (STIC tasks) so that your child builds his or her experience confronting and coping with stress. The therapist may also want to arrange therapy sessions at your child's school or in places other than the office to conduct assisted in vivo practices. Over time, your child will learn to construct and carry out his or her own exposures and turn anxiety-provoking situations into positive opportunities to take on challenges. The main goal is to train your child to recognize when negative emotions occur, and then to immediately set up an exposure and take coping action rather than avoiding or escaping. This coping process is termed "transfer of control" (Silverman & Kurtines, 1996). In the transfer of control model, the therapist is the expert who assumes responsibility during treatment to transfer his or her knowledge of coping with negative emotions to you and your child. The therapist does this by modeling for and training you to conduct in-vivo desensitization at home, and helping your child practice anxiety management skills. Through systematic homework assignments, you become an active and crucial part of the transfer process by fostering your child's sense of control and mastery of negative emotions.

Review of Assigned In Vivo Desensitization and STIC Tasks

Each session will begin with a review of the assigned homework and an examination of your child's progress during in vivo desensitization practices (STIC tasks). Examples of assigned tasks include visiting the school and/or teacher, staying alone for increasingly longer periods, and approaching and remaining in other situations. The therapist will help your child troubleshoot any difficulties during these in vivo practices. The therapist will emphasize the importance of using relaxation and deep breathing techniques to remain calm during difficult situations and to stay in a situation rather than avoiding or escaping. In addition, the therapist will review your child's progress in adhering to a school schedule and his or her initial attempts at attending classes or school functions.

Stepping Up the STIC Tasks: Eliminating Safety Signals

As treatment continues, your child will confront more challenging situations for in vivo desensitization both within and between sessions. One focus of your child's desensitization practices should be to enter difficult situations without help or the use of "safety signals." A safety signal is any object or person that your child relies on to feel better or less anxious in a situation. Although a safety signal may lessen your child's anxiety in the short-term, the long-term use of safety signals maintains anxiety and prevents your child from learning that he or she can manage the situation.

When your child is worried, fearful, anxious, or sad, he or she may become more clingy or needy of attention and reassurance. Children who refuse to attend school or other activities due to these negative emotions can often be "bribed" into entering these situations with assistance. For example, some anxious children will only ride the school bus if a certain sibling or friend accompanies them. If the "safety" child is absent, the anxious child more strongly resists riding the bus. Similarly, children with panic disorder may require elaborate safety measures, such as carrying a cellular telephone in case they need to call for help. Children with panic disorder find it very difficult to be away from home or their primary caretaker for fear that no one else will understand or be able to help them if a panic attack occurs.

Increasing the complexity and challenge of the STIC tasks is important to uncover, and then dispose of, as many of these unnecessary and unhelpful safety signals as possible. Table 4.1 lists some common safety signals for children who refuse school. The therapist will help your child construct in vivo practices to confront and challenge these negative emotions. As each practice progresses, accompanying safety signals will be systematically taken away so that your child has the opportunity to learn how to manage the situation alone.

Table 4.1. Negative Emotions and Behaviors and Accompanying Safety Signals

Negative Emotions and Behaviors	Safety Signals
Worry: "What if" thinking; reassurance-seeking; anxiety in new or changing situations; perfectionism.	Repeated questioning; needing to know every detail and plan; carrying everything in the book bag (fear of leaving something behind); rewriting and erasing to get a paper "perfect."
Panic: Anxiety about the sudden rush of certain body sensations, such as a racing heart, sweating, dizziness, shortness of breath, or shaking.	Having someone always close by "just in case" (e.g., friend, parent); carrying certain objects to feel better (e.g., water, medicine, cellular telephones or beepers); checking heartbeat or pulse; dropping out of sports or gym activities.
Anxiety about specific objects or situations: Anxiety about fire drills, riding the bus, insects or animals, thunderstorms, a ringing bell, small places like classrooms, doctors, needles, or the dark.	Watching a weather report and anticipating a storm; sleeping with the lights on or needing someone to sleep with the child; earplugs.
Separation anxiety concerns: Anxiety that something terrible will happen when separated from home or loved ones, and then two people will never see each other again.	"Shadowing" or clinging to Mom or Dad; always being in sight of Mom or Dad; never being alone; needing lots of reassurance if a separation is going to occur.
Sadness, the "blues," or depression: Being down more days than not; feeling hopeless or that things will never work out; feelings of worthlessness or guilt; loss of interest in usual activities; irritability; crying; thoughts of death or harming self.	Clinging; not wanting to be alone; having someone else (parent, friend) solve or handle one's problems due to beliefs that "I can't ever get things right" or "I don't deserve this."

Example In Vivo Practices

Increasing the challenge of the STIC tasks, along with decreasing the use of safety signals, will give your child experience with managing difficult situations. The therapist may begin with an imaginal desensitization so that your child is prepared for the in vivo practice situation. The therapist will describe your child confronting a stressful situation and *not* engaging in a safety behavior. If your child progresses fairly rapidly, then in vivo desensitization may begin quickly. The following are examples of in vivo desensitization plans for three of the most common forms of distress among children with school refusal behavior.

Example 1: The Clinging Child–"Don't leave me alone!"

Problem focus: Anxiety about something terrible happening to Mom or Dad, or of being kidnapped or killed, or of getting lost and not being able to find the way home.

Safety behaviors and signals: Needing to call home every hour during the school day; needing Mom and Dad to call home every hour when they go out without the children; having Mom or Dad always arrive early to pick up child from school; having Mom or Dad drive down the same streets to prevent getting lost.

In vivo desensitization plans: The child will practice going for increasingly longer periods of time without talking to Mom or Dad, and gradually work up to not knowing their whereabouts. Telephone calls initially can be stretched to every 90 minutes, then to twice in the morning and once in the afternoon, then to once only in the morning, and then to no calls at all. A similar schedule would apply when the parents go out without the children: call home every 90 minutes, then every 2 hours, then once during any four-hour period, and then not at all.

In vivo practice for anxieties about not being picked up on time will have a parent arrive 5 minutes late and give a plausible excuse (e.g., stuck in traffic), then 10 minutes late with an excuse, then 10 minutes late without an excuse, and then 20 minutes late (working up to 45 minutes). To increase the challenge in this situation, the therapist may employ "confederates," or assistants who are unknown to the child, who will walk by or ask for directions. Concurrently with this type of exposure, the therapist will instruct the child about what to do to stay safe if a parent is running late: wait inside the school building and inform the office staff that you are there; stay outside and inform a teacher or an adult who is well-known that you are waiting for your parents; do not approach strangers; if a stranger approaches you, walk quickly toward a group of kids, an adult who you know, or someone in authority such as a police officer or crossing guard. The goal of this type of exposure is to enhance the child's tolerance for normal inconveniences and to develop the necessary skills to manage and remain safe in an ambiguous situation.

To desensitize anxiety about getting lost, the therapist and parent may blindfold the child (using a mask or scarf) and, without talking, take the child on a walk around the office building or outside area. Although the child is being led by the hand, the absence of conversation and not being able to see the surroundings will arouse anxiety and worry. By increasing the practice time, the child will again learn to tolerate an ambiguous situation. In the next step, the parents will drive on unfamiliar roads and occasionally mumble "Oh boy, where are we?" The parents are instructed not to give any reassurance to the child and stay "lost" for increasing periods. The parent will then verbalize his or her plan for finding the correct street while remaining calm and in control: "Okay, let's see where we are. Breathe slowly, relax. This is Hylan Boulevard, and I know that it runs into

New Dorp Lane at some point. Take it easy, stay calm and relaxed. I'll keep driving in this direction for another mile. Okay! There's New Dorp Lane! I knew I could find it if I just remained calm!"

Example 2: Pushing the Panic Button–"I feel sick and I need help!"

Problem focus: Panic attacks occur in a variety of situations or places, and may cause nausea, dizziness, shortness of breath, heart palpitations, sweating, shaking, numbing or tingling sensations, and feelings of unreality. These attacks may have come "from out of the blue" or may have happened to the child in school, on the bus, in public places such as malls and movie theaters, and/or in crowds.

Safety behaviors and signals: Carrying a paper bag in case of hyperventilation, a bottle of water to keep the throat "open," and a cellular telephone to call for help; needing to have Mom available by telephone at all times; parents rearranging their work schedules to drive the child to and from school to avoid the bus that "triggers my panic attacks"; attending school only for half days because panic is more likely to occur in the afternoon; staying home to rest in bed each afternoon to stave off panic; being given an open pass by the teacher to go to the school nurse at any time during class in case of panic symptoms (on average, spending at least 1 hour each morning with the nurse), and then lying on a cot.

In vivo desensitization plans: For a child who experiences panic attacks, interoceptive exposure exercises help desensitize him or her to the physical sensations that accompany panic. Interoceptive conditioning is the process of learning to be afraid of physical sensations. Individuals who experience panic begin to feel a change in their physical state and become very vigilant about the change and afraid of its implications. They thus typically avoid running up stairs, aerobic activity, drinking caffeinated beverages, or other situations or activities that may cause physical changes. One key to overcoming panic is to learn to tolerate normal physical arousal and changes without becoming frightened and distressed. Interoceptive exposure involves the systematic provocation of these sensations over repeated trials to reduce anxiety. A hierarchy of sensations that frighten the child is constructed, and, beginning with the least anxiety-provoking sensation, the child engages in exercises designed to elicit the sensation at higher and higher intensities. Typical exercises and their targets are listed in Table 4.2.

Table 4.2. Interoceptive Exposure

Exercise	Target Sensation
Spinning in a chair	Dizziness, lightheadedness
Running in place or up stairs	Shortness of breath, racing/pounding heart
Breathing through a straw	Shortness of breath, chest tightness
Staring at a light and then reading	Visual disturbances, unreality
Shaking head from side to side	Lightheadedness
Tensing all muscles, and holding them very tight	Muscle tension, tingling sensations
Hyperventilation	Shortness of breath, pounding heart, lightheadedness, tingling sensations
Putting head down below the knees, and then "popping" up very quickly	Lightheadedness, dizziness, unreality

The goal of having the child engage in these exercises is to teach him or her that these sensations are temporary, predictable, and controllable. Most importantly, the child learns that changes in physical states are normal and harmless. Parents should be forewarned that the child will be somewhat uncomfortable, but only temporarily. The sensations of a panic attack are harmless and will eventually go away even if the child does nothing at all. Most importantly, the child will learn that normal functioning does not have to be changed because he or she experiences panic attacks.

The child should also be entering situations that he or she avoids and gradually leave safety signals (e.g., paper bags, cellular telephones, water bottles) at home. School attendance should be gradually increased and visits to the nurse more limited. These steps involve cooperation with the teacher and school nurse, so the therapist must be able to communicate how they may coach the child to comply with the desensitization. Similarly, practice at home will involve spending less time in bed and increasing the amount of time spent engaging in physical activities (e.g., bike riding) that arouse physical sensations. The child should use deep breathing whenever anxiety is aroused, and to remain in the situation despite feeling panic-like sensations.

Example 3: The Worrier-"What if, what if, what if?"

Problem focus: Excessive worry about new situations, changes in routine, or doing things perfectly or to an unrealistic standard; difficulty with concentration, resting and sleeping well; complaints of muscle tension or aches; and repeatedly asking the same question.

Safety behaviors and signals: Constantly seeking reassurance from parents, teachers, and peers; teacher reporting that the child is "always at my desk"; child needing to know what the family's plan is for every day of the week and having difficulty if plans are changed or unexpected events occur.

In vivo desensitization plans: The child will be taught to experience less than perfect or desired circumstances, and accept the consequences without asking for reassurance. For example, a child who is a perfectionist and puts undue pressure on himself or herself may be asked to purposefully make mistakes on homework papers or in sporting activities (e.g., strike out in baseball). Similarly, a child who is overly preoccupied with looking perfect may be asked to wear something wrinkled, have messed up hair, and not use the mirror to check on his or her appearance. Reassurance should not be given. Parents must refrain from responding to the child when he or she repeatedly asks "Do you think this is okay?" When the in vivo desensitization involves making mistakes on schoolwork, ask the teacher to expect a change in the child's work, and possibly prepare some worksheets that will not enter into the child's official grade. The child will be taught that, even if mistakes occur, there are usually no long-term consequences and most mistakes can be remedied.

A child who is overly concerned with details of plans and activities will be taught to confront unknown and changing experiences. A parent may schedule an outing that involves several planned stops (e.g., first to the mall, then to Grandma's house, then to the library). Typically, children who worry excessively will want to know all of the details of each stop, such as how long they will be there, what will happen, and who else may be involved. The parent then changes the order of the plans (e.g., go to Grandma's first) and length of time that the child expects to be in each place (e.g., leaving ahead of schedule or staying longer in one place). As the child begins to adjust, the parent advances desensitization by confronting established expectations (e.g., Grandma is not at home, the library is closed) and canceling an individual element of the plan. Last, the parent cancels an entire scheduled outing at the last minute, without giving notice to the child.

The Ups and Downs of Providing Reassurance

As a parent, your natural tendency is to comfort your child when he or she is upset, protect your child from harm and stress, and give your child experiences that enhance his or her self-esteem and development. It is perfectly natural and normal for you to respond to tears and fears with hugs and comforting words. It is also normal for your child to ask questions about events and daily life situations, especially as he or she grows and gains more experience with the larger world.

Children who are prone to experience anxiety or distress, however, can push you to your limits. This is not the child's fault, nor is it yours. Some people are more inclined to respond to stress with depression, anxiety, and fear. For example, take a moment to think about different relatives or friends. Imagine how each would respond to hearing that he or she may be laid off from his or her jobs. Some may react with anger and punch the wall. Some may react with depression and withdraw. Some may start worrying and thinking about all the terrible things that could result from the layoff. Finally, some may start planning for the layoff and evaluating how they could deal with the situation. Each person reacts with some degree of guidance from his or her temperament. Every person is born with a temperament that guides him or her toward being more angry, depressed, anxious, fearful, excitable, low-key, or "even-keeled."

Individuals born with anxious and depressive temperaments may learn over time to respond to situations with increasing distress. This is where your child's anxious or depressive temperament can interact in a negative way with your parenting practices. When your child is upset, you want to provide comfort. Parents of anxious or depressed children find that they provide much more comfort and reassurance than they do for their children with more even temperaments. They also notice differences between how they react to their distressed child and how other parents react to their children. Moreover, parents of distressed children learn over time that they never seem able to provide enough reassurance or comfort for their child. The distress continues, the questioning doesn't seem to end, and the parent's frustration level is reached more and more quickly with every life event. This is a paradox: as a parent, you want to comfort your child; because of your child's distressed temperament, however, you may never have enough comfort to satisfy his or her needs. As a result, you may become resentful or frustrated with your child, and you dread the confrontations that result from his or her unending or unrealistic needs. Finally, you may feel guilty or inadequate as a parent.

You have done nothing wrong. Your child's school refusal behavior and accompanying distress is a result of his or her temperament interacting with his or her life experiences and your desire to be a good parent. In plain terms, there is no one to blame and no reason to look for blame. Your child has learned over time to react in certain ways, and you have learned to react to your child with increasing levels of reassurance and comfort. The key to helping your child cope with and manage his or her distress, however, is to stop providing reassurance and comfort beyond what you would give to the average child.

Through this program of relaxation training and desensitization, your child will learn to accept the ups and downs of everyday life. Also, your child will learn to comfort himself or herself when feeling normal levels of arousal or distress and to use appropriate coping skills to enter and deal with various situations at school and home. For your child to succeed in this program, you should follow the therapist's feedback. You will learn to provide reassurance when it is appropriate, and ignore complaints and tears when there is nothing real to be upset over or if your child's distress is excessive. The in vivo desensitization plans are designed to expose your child to what he or she fears or dreads and teach your child that he or she can handle the situation. Your child may become somewhat upset when entering school situations that he or she has avoided for a period of time. If you provide too much reassurance, however, and allow your child to escape or avoid the in vivo desensitization practices, then he or she will receive the message that he or she can't handle the situation. Only with experience will your child learn to master these negative emotions. You have to be prepared to let your child feel some distress until he or she learns that nothing is going to happen that he or she can't deal with in some way.

Guidelines for Providing Reassurance

If your child asks a question, answer one time. If he or she asks again, remind him or her that he or she knows the answer, but remind calmly and only once. If asked again, turn away from your child. Example:

C: When do I have to start going to school?

P: You'll start on Monday, with social studies class. (Ten minutes or so pass.)

C: Do I have to start going to school on Monday?

P: You know the answer to that question.

C: But, is it this coming Monday, is that when?

(Turn away from child. When your child begins to speak about other topics, or continues on a more appropriate discussion regarding school, turn back to your child and continue to give attention.)

If your child is going to attempt an in vivo desensitization task that is new or particularly challenging, direct him or her to use the relaxation and deep breathing skills learned in therapy. Remind your child once about his or her accomplishments up to this point. Do not dwell on the issue, and do not get into a long discussion where you are providing too much comfort and reassurance.

C: I don't think I can stay in school all day. What if I don't feel well and want to come home?

P: Why don't you look over your logbooks and notes from therapy? Think about all the things you've been doing that you couldn't do before.

C: Yeah, I know. But that's different. Dr. Eisen was always there. Now I have to go all day by myself.

P: It sounds to me as though you should practice your deep breathing and relaxation some more.

C: But what if I forget to do this in school? What will happen if I get really sick or something? I don't know if I should go on Monday.

P: The plan is set for Monday, and you're going to go to school. You know what to do to help yourself, and it's time to do it. (Parent turns away.)

Give your child attention for appropriate behavior, positive coping, and practicing the skills learned in therapy. The key is to reinforce your child when he or she is sticking with the program and to ignore negative behaviors.

P: Hey, I heard you playing your STIC tape just now. What's up?

C: Dr. Eisen said I should practice each day, and imagine myself going to school for longer and longer times.

P: I'm very proud of you for following what Dr. Eisen says to do. I know it hasn't been easy for you. You should feel really good about yourself, for making yourself to go to school and do all this work. What are the things that are easier for you to do now?

(Parent and child continue to discuss progress, and the positive ways the child has coped with distressing situations. The child gains attention for talking about his or her efforts at coping.)

The therapist may ask you to join the sessions to practice ignoring inappropriate behavior and to give positive attention for appropriate behavior. The therapist will also discuss ways you can help your child with the in vivo desensitization plans.

Homework

Homework assignments after sessions 5–6 may include the following:

- Continue to practice the relaxation tape at bedtime and complete logbooks.
- Complete STIC tasks that will involve various in vivo desensitization plans, in addition to imaginal desensitization as needed.
- Increase attendance at school over the course of these sessions, with the goal of having your child attend most of the day, every day.
- Continue to complete the daily logbooks, noting any specific issues or situations that arise during the week.

Sessions 7–8: Completing Treatment

By this point in your child's program, he or she will be expected to attend school on a full-time basis. The therapist may have helped your child return to school by actually going in with him or her the first few times. It is important that children who are sensitive to general distress continue to use the relaxation and deep breathing skills they learned early in the program. These skills will prove invaluable when your child confronts a stressor or anxious situation in real life. The purpose of the in vivo desensitization and exposure STIC tasks has been to prepare your child for confrontations and to give him or her practice in managing emotions during these times. Most importantly, the STIC tasks have been designed to gradually bring your child to full-time school attendance and tapered support from the therapist. Your child is now in the end stages of the transfer of control approach. He or she should be taking most of the responsibility for the treatment process and applying what was learned in real-life situations. If necessary, the therapist will continue to implement techniques from previous sessions to help your child achieve this goal.

Children Refusing School to Escape Painful Social and/or Evaluative Situations

Session 1: Starting Treatment

Many people can recall when being in a social situation, being the focus of attention, or being tested or evaluated was accompanied by butterflies, shaking, or some other indication of anxiety. For most people, these initial feelings of anxiety disappear quickly, and their ability to perform in the social or evaluative situation is not impaired. Many people can also recall times during their school years when being called on in class to give an oral report, being teased by others, or taking a test would trigger those physical sensations that signal anxiety. For some children, anxiety in social and evaluative situations is so distressing that they cannot tolerate these situations. Instead, avoidance behavior takes over. If your child refuses school to escape painful social and evaluative situations, treatment will involve:

- identifying what your child tells himself or herself in anxiety-provoking situations,
- changing negative thoughts to coping, helpful statements,
- developing graduated exposure to anxiety-provoking social and/or evaluative situations in session, and
- practicing coping skills in real-life social and/or evaluative situations.

The therapist will spend the majority of each session with your child, but will invite you to the last part of each session to give your input, review material covered in that session, and plan homework. If your child has been avoiding social situations such as attending parties, initiating or joining conversations, or talking on the telephone, the therapist will show you how to help your child enter those situations. Similarly, if your child has had difficulty with evaluative or performance situations, he or she will learn to engage in those situations in a graduated and structured manner. It will be your task, under the guidance of the therapist, to facilitate your child's contact with these situations.

Psychoeducation

The therapist will begin treatment by helping your child understand the nature and process of social and evaluative anxiety. Anxiety is divided into three components: physical (*What I feel*), cognitive (*What I think*), and behavioral (*What I do*). The following is an example of how a therapist might explain to your child how the interaction of these components maintains anxiety:

> Do you remember what it was like the first time you tried to ride a bicycle? Think back to how you felt getting on the bike for the first time. Were you able to just jump on it and ride away, or did you feel shaky and think that you might fall? Remember how it was to have someone hold onto the seat, to steady you? What did you think would happen if they let go of the seat and left you to go on your own? Well,

with practice, again and again, you learned to feel comfortable and ride that bike straight and steady. Do you think about how scared you were whenever you jump on a bike now? Of course not! Because you got used to riding the bike, now you don't even notice if you feel a little shaky at first.

Now, what do you think would have happened if, that first time you were on a bike, feeling all shaky, you got off the bike and never got back on it again? What if you told yourself, *This is too scary, I may fall, and then I could get hurt.* Do you think you would've wanted to jump back onto that bike again? No way! If you tell yourself that something is scary, and that you can't do something, then it really feels scary and it keeps you from wanting to try again. This is the same thing that happens to some people when they have to give an oral report, or play an instrument in front of other people, or take a test in school, or even when they try to start conversations. Because they tell themselves that it's a scary situation, and that they can feel shaky or butterflies or such, then they don't want to do those things anymore. And, the more they avoid those things, the worse it can get. That's because they feel more afraid than they really would be in that situation.

The therapist may draw three circles, each depicting a component of anxiety, and ask your child to identify his or her own physical feelings, thoughts, and behaviors when confronted with a social-anxiety situation. The therapist may use cartoons or pictures from magazines depicting children in various situations (e.g., standing near a group of children, talking with an adult), and your child will be asked to describe what the child in the picture may be feeling, thinking, and doing. In this way, the therapist and your child can build rapport, understand what provokes anxiety, and understand how your child interprets various situations. The therapist can illustrate to your child the process of escalating anxiety, and the opposite process of calming or de-escalation.

Building an Anxiety and Avoidance Hierarchy

Using information gathered from the assessment interviews and logbooks, the therapist will help your child build his or her Anxiety and Avoidance Hierarchy (AAH; see Figure A.5). This is a list of situations that the therapist and your child will target for change over the course of treatment. Using a Feelings Thermometer (see Figure A.6) or other measurement scale, your child will rate his or her anxiety and avoidance of these situations at each session. The therapist may also ask for your input when building the AAH.

Figure 5.1 shows a sample AAH of a twelve-year-old boy who refused to attend school due to anxiety about social and evaluative situations. As you can see, steps on the AAH are gradual so Mark can begin with the easiest (or lowest) item and

Anxiety and Avoidance Hierarchy

Problem: *School refusal due to anxiety about social or evaluative situations*

Situations or Places That Scare Me!	Anxiety Rating	Avoidance Rating
1. *Starting a conversation with two kids I don't know well*	8	8
2. *Going to the lunch room, and sitting with some kids I don't know too well*	8	7
3. *Volunteering to read out loud or write on the blackboard*	7	7
4. *Calling up someone from class and asking about the homework*	7	7
5. *Raising my hand to answer a question*	6	7
6. *Giving an oral report*	6	6
7. *Answering and talking on the telephone when it rings at home*	5	4
8. *Asking the teacher for help or to explain something*	4	4
9. *Ordering my own food in the cafeteria or a restaurant*	4	4
10. *Starting a conversation with someone I know*	3	3

Figure 5.1. **Mark's Anxiety and Avoidance Hierarchy**

progress to the most difficult (highest) hierarchy item. This is how your child's treatment will proceed.

Identifying Negative Thoughts

Anxiety about social and evaluative situations is largely a result of negative thoughts or "self-talk." When anticipating a social or evaluative situation, your child is likely to focus on what could go wrong, how bad he or she may look, or on the belief that others will laugh or think badly of him or her. During these situations, your child may focus on these negative thoughts instead of on how the situation is really progressing. As a result, anxiety increases and can overwhelm your child. The therapist will help your child develop a plan to identify and change these negative thoughts.

If your child is a younger child, the therapist may use the letters S-T-O-P to help change negative thoughts (Silverman & Kurtines, 1996):

S stands for: Are you feeling **Scared**?

T stands for: What are you **Thinking**?

O points you towards **Other Helpful Thoughts**

P is to **Praise** yourself for using these steps, and **Plan** for the next time.

Depending on your child's age and developmental level, the therapist may rehearse these steps sequentially with your child, focusing on using the steps in different social or evaluative situations that may trigger anxious thoughts. However, it is not critical that your child learn the steps in detail. In fact, younger children and those with limited cognitive abilities respond well to a picture of a STOP sign, which can be used as a signal to "stop and think" when confronting an anxiety-provoking situation (see Figure 5.2).

Figure 5.2. STOP Illustration

If your child is older, or is an adolescent, the therapist will help him or her identify "Automatic Thoughts," or ATs. ATs are negative, unhelpful, anxious thoughts that seem to happen automatically and focus on what is dangerous or frightening about a situation. In fact, ATs can make a benign situation seem very frightening. Examples of common ATs are:

All or None Thinking: It must be perfect. I can't do this at all.

Catastrophizing: This is the worst thing that can happen to me.

Can'ts or Shoulds: I can't ever get this right. I can't do this. I should have done better.

Mind Reading: She thinks I'm stupid. I know they don't like me.

Fortune Telling: I'm going to fail this test. Nobody will talk to me.

Canceling the positive (usually occurs when someone gives a compliment): I should have done better. This wasn't my best work.

In session 1, your child will learn to identify his or her thoughts in those situations that trigger anxiety. Step one will be to teach your child to recognize the cues, or "triggers," for his or her anxiety (focus is on the "S" step). Younger children will be asked to draw pictures of those things that cause anxiety. Older children will be asked to keep a logbook or list of situations that cause anxiety. You can help the therapist identify these cues by keeping a logbook of situations where you notice that your child's avoidance or other behavior is signaling anxiety. You should keep your list separate from your child's, and it is best to not prompt your child or compare lists. The therapist will use the lists to help your child identify how he or she anticipates and predicts negative events.

The Coaching Team

When you are invited into the session, the therapist will have your child review the day's progress. It will be helpful for you to follow your child through the process of challenging and changing negative thoughts so that you can "coach" your child during tough situations.

A sports team analogy illustrates how to assist your child. Your child is told that he or she is the "quarterback" or "point guard" of the team. The therapist is the "head coach" and the parents are the "sideline coaches." At first, the head coach calls all the plays. The head coach lays out the STOP plan for challenging and changing negative thoughts, and sets up the initial role-play exposures to practice managing anxiety. As sideline coaches, you will help your child set up home-based practices. As sideline coaches you will also study the plays (STOP plan) and assist your child as needed. The therapist will instruct you to prompt your child to use the STOP steps. As the "game" (treatment) progresses session by session, the head coach will let the quarterback call some of his or her own plays. The whole team will assist at first but, as the quarterback gets to really understand the plays, he or she can begin to call them alone. This analogy illustrates the process of helping your child learn the anxiety management skills and exposure plans, and the process of setting up the initial exposures. However, with time and practice, your child will assume greater responsibility for his or her own therapy.

Homework

Homework assignments after session 1 may include the following:

- You and your child should each keep a separate log of situations that cause your child anxiety.
- Continue to complete the daily logbooks, noting any specific issues or situations that arise during the week.

Session 2: Intensifying Treatment

In this session, the therapist will begin with a continued focus on your child's self-talk. Specifically, he or she will teach your child to identify and dispute negative, unhelpful thoughts. The therapist will use behavioral exposures to prompt your child's anxiety reactions and then his or her use of coping self-talk skills. In a behavioral exposure, the therapist and your child will role-play an anxiety-producing situation, such as starting a conversation with someone in the cafeteria. The purpose of this role-play is to prompt your child to experience anxiety and to identify his or her negative thoughts that perpetuate the anxiety. The therapist will then help your child dispute these thoughts. Moreover, behavioral exposure will allow your child to practice gradually entering those situations that cause anxiety; therefore, he or she can gain experience with approach and mastery of these situations. Real-life (in vivo) practice in entering these situations will occur between sessions, with your assistance. These real-life practices are called "Show That I Can," or STIC tasks (Kendall et al., 1992). STIC tasks are designed to reinforce and extend the treatment techniques introduced during the session. The therapist will help you set up and conduct these STIC tasks.

Challenging and Changing Negative Thoughts

The therapist will review the past week with your child, and focus on identifying the triggers of his or her anxiety as well as corresponding negative thoughts and images. Using a chalkboard or flip chart, the therapist will help your child identify his or her specific patterns of arousal and negative thoughts (see Figure 5.3). The following is an example of dialogue that may accompany this exercise. In the dialogue, **T** represents the therapist and **C** represents the child.

T: So, one of the things that happened last week was that you walked out to the playground, and a bunch of kids were already playing a game. This made you nervous?

C: Yeah, I was upset.

T: Okay, so the "trigger" was seeing a group of kids playing a game. Let's write that up here on the board, and call it the trigger. Okay, so think about what was going on right before you saw the kids. You were walking out of the school, headed toward the playground. What were you thinking?

C: I don't know. I wanted to go out and play.

T: Okay, so you wanted to go play. Did you think about what game you wanted to play, or who you might play with?

C: Yeah, I thought I'd play tag with my friend Bethany. I was looking for her.

T: Okay, and how were you feeling right then, before you got out onto the playground?

C: I wanted to play, and was glad it was recess. I felt happy.

T: Then you see the kids playing together. What did you notice then?

C: Bethany was out there with a bunch of kids playing. I got nervous.

T: All right, that's the "S" in STOP. Let's put that on the board. When you say that you saw Bethany with a bunch of kids, that's when you first noticed that you were scared. Now, what were you thinking?

C: I don't really ever play with those kids. Bethany may not want to play with me. What if they don't want to play with me? (The therapist will write these thoughts on the board under "T".)

T: Okay, let's look at these thoughts that you are having. One at a time we'll look at each. Start with "I don't ever play with those kids." Do you remember back before you use to play with Bethany? Before you knew her?

C: Yes, in first grade.

T: Were you afraid to go and play with her, when you first saw her?

C: A little. But we started playing together. And it was okay.

T: So once you started playing together, you were less and less scared?

C: Yeah, I wasn't scared of her anymore. We became friends then.

T: Right! There's always a time when we haven't done something, but once we do it, it gets easier. So, what other things can you say to yourself instead of "I never play with those kids"?

C: Well, I haven't played with them before, but I could get to play with them and know them. (The therapist writes these thoughts on the board under "O".)

T: Great! That is a really helpful thought, and gives you a good plan for what to do.

Trigger	**S**cared?	**T**houghts?	**O**ther, helpful thoughts?	**P**raise!
Recess	*Seeing Bethany playing with a bunch of kids.*	*I don't ever play with them. Bethany may not want to play with me.* *What if they don't want to play with me?*	*I haven't played with them before, but I could try and get to know them!*	*This is a good plan for me!*

Figure 5.3. **STOP Example**

The therapist will lead your child through each negative thought and ask about his or her experience with similar situations. This process will teach your child to examine the evidence for these thoughts and to dispute the thoughts with rational, realistic thinking. The following questions (termed "dispute handles"; Beck, Rush, Shaw, & Emery, 1979) are commonly used to refute anxious thoughts:

Am I 100% sure this will happen?

Can I really know what that person thinks of me?

What's the worse thing that can really happen?

Have I ever been in a situation like this before, and was it really that bad?

How many times has this terrible thing actually happened?

So what if I don't get a perfect grade on this test?

Am I the only person that has ever had to deal with this situation?

The therapist and your child will go through several examples of STOP to practice challenging and changing these negative thoughts. This will prepare your child for the next section of the session, behavioral exposure.

Tracking Anxiety During Behavioral Exposure

Prior to the start of your child's role-play, the therapist will ask for a rating of anxiety. This is your child's best estimate of how nervous or anxious he or she feels. The therapist will ask your child to rate his or her level of anxiety using the Feelings Thermometer or other measurement scale. Anxiety ratings will then be taken every minute during the behavioral exposure role-play. Most behavioral exposures last 10–15 minutes. The therapist will record your child's ratings throughout treatment. Also, prior to the exposure, the therapist will ask your child to define several specific goals for the exposure. These goals will be concrete, observable, and attainable behaviors or actions that your child will work toward performing. For example, in an exposure focused on starting and maintaining a conversation, a child may have the following goals: I will introduce myself and say hello, I will ask two questions, I will look up and make good eye contact during the conversation.

The therapist will also keep track of whether your child meets these goals during the exposure role-play. After the role-play, the therapist will discuss with your child how he or she feels, and whether he or she thinks the goals were met. Using graphics on a flip chart or board, the therapist will present your child's anxiety ratings and put up the "score" for each goal. At this point, the therapist will process the exposure with your child, focusing on his or her behavior, whether the anxiety interfered with performance, and whether your child was able to use the STOP procedures to change any negative thoughts. They will then discuss strategies for building on the successes and overcoming any trouble encountered during the exposure. The main lesson in this process is that practice helps and that anxiety will naturally go away as your child learns to focus on the situation instead of his or her feelings.

Some children are able to track their own anxiety levels. Recording their own ratings gives children instant information about how they handled a certain situation. The ratings can illustrate how they coped with any situation where anxiety ratings can be taken and recorded. You may wish to keep your child's ratings in a log or notebook to remind your child of progress made during therapy.

Initial Behavioral Exposures

The therapist will help your child choose a relatively easy situation from his or her AAH. Through the use of role-playing, the therapist and your child will create the situation in the session,. allowing your child to practice the STOP procedures. Behavioral exposures serve several purposes in your child's treatment. They allow him or her to practice anxiety management skills while approaching and engaging in situations he or she normally avoids. Instead of responding to normal levels of anxiety by trying to escape or avoid, your child will learn to tolerate normal rises in anxiety and allow these feelings to go away naturally while remaining in the situation. Behavioral exposures allow your child to gain mastery and control over his or her anxiety.

Another way of understanding the therapeutic process involved in behavioral exposures is to think about a social or evaluative situation that would cause anyone to feel anxious. For example, if you imagine yourself back in school, think about what might go through your mind as you wait for the teacher to call on you to give an oral report. Anyone who has given an oral report can recall butterflies in the stomach, sweaty hands, shaky voice, and sweating. As the teacher calls each of your classmates to talk, you wait for your turn, look at the clock, and think "I hope I don't have to go today; Hurry up and ring the bell; What if I don't know what to say?" If the bell rings and class ends before your turn, recall what happens to the feelings and thoughts of anxiety. They typically go away immediately. This immediate relief serves to reinforce anxiety in the long run, and for those individuals who are prone to being anxious, the pattern of escape or avoiding anxiety can begin. For these people, at the next initial sign of anxiety (e.g., butterflies or a "What if" thought), they are more likely to want to avoid the situation (e.g., stay home with complaints of being sick) or escape (e.g., leave school sick). However, those people who attend the next class and sit waiting for their turn are likely to gain experience with the situation and learn a different lesson.

Recall what actually happens when giving an oral report. Although anxious at first, over time most people learn that the initial rise of sensations goes away by itself. These are temporary feelings that anyone can experience when anticipating something or getting "psyched up" to do an activity. Moreover, with repeated experience and talking with peers and family members, people learn that everyone feels these things at times, that these thoughts and feelings are normal, and that, in spite of these feelings, they can still perform and master the task.

Processing Exposures

Throughout the course of treatment, the therapist will give your child feedback about what happened to his or her anxiety during the exposure practices. The therapist will illustrate the process of mastering anxiety and negative feelings by drawing graphs or diagrams of your child's anxiety ratings. This will show how your child's anxiety dissipated in each exposure practice (see example in Figure 5.4).

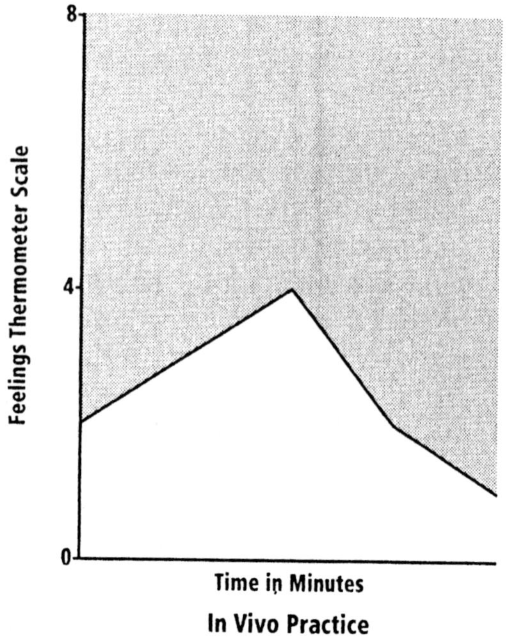

Figure 5.4. **Mark's Anxiety Rating**

If your child's anxiety ratings do not readily habituate (go down), the therapist will process with your child what thoughts he or she may be having during the exposure. For especially troublesome or negative thoughts, procedures for identifying and changing negative thoughts will continue to be used. These procedures will increase your child's ability to identify and change negative thoughts.

Setting the Pace of, and Assistance With, Exposures

There are several ways to conduct practices to set the pace of role-play (and later in vivo) exposures. Gradual exposure occurs at a relatively slow pace set by the therapist and your child. The therapist will set a slower pace for younger children, those with special needs, and those with exceptionally high levels of anxiety. The rationale for moving slower is to allow the child to fully handle anxiety, overlearn the plan of confronting the stressor, and build the child's trust that he or she will not be forced into something overwhelming.

In assisted exposure, either you or the therapist performs the exposure with your child. Your child can learn by example and feel supported when overcoming his or her anxieties. A careful balance must be struck between *modeling,* where you show the child how to manage the situation, and *rescuing,* where you take over and manage the situation for your child. Modeling and assisted exposure keep the focus on your child. The goal is for your child to confront the stressor and manage the situation himself or herself. Typically, the therapist first models for your child how to deal with the situation while your child observes. Next, the therapist helps the child manage the situation. The child and therapist (or parent) then engage in the situation as a team. Next, the child manages the situation on his or her own, with words of encouragement from the therapist or parent. Finally, the child engages the situation on his or her own while verbalizing self-reinforcement for performing the exposure.

Homework

Homework assignments after session 2 may involve the following:

- Write down your child's thoughts during anxiety-provoking situations. Following the STOP model, your child will be required to identify and change his or her negative thoughts.
- The therapist will ask your child to practice in real life the situation role-played during this session (STIC task). Your child will be required to practice at least three times prior to the next session. For example, if his or her difficulty involves calling a classmate on the telephone, the assignment will be to call a classmate(s) three times during the week. Your child will also be asked to record an anxiety rating immediately prior to, and immediately after, this exercise. You are encouraged to talk with your child after each practice, much like the therapist would during a session, and focus your child on what really occurred during the practice and what happened to the anxiety. Praise and encourage each attempted and completed practice.
- Wake your child about 90–120 minutes before school is scheduled to start and follow the normal school-day routine. Follow this routine as closely as possible. During the day, your child should do schoolwork and read school-related books if he or she stays home.
- Continue to complete the daily logbooks, noting any specific issues or situations that arise during the week.

Sessions 3–4: Maturing of Treatment

In session 2, the therapist continued to help your child challenge and change negative thoughts. In addition, your child practiced role-plays (behavioral exposures) of troublesome situations. Sessions 3–4 will begin with a review of your child's STIC tasks and a discussion of any difficulties in conducting and following through with the homework. The therapist may decide to role-play any difficulties encountered by your child since the last session, including any troubles that may have occurred during the STIC exposures. The main focus of these sessions will be to prompt your child to confront more challenging social situations. Again, this will be enhanced by role-playing these situations with the therapist. To facilitate your child's challenging and changing of negative thoughts, and to reinforce coping with difficult situations, the therapist will make these role-plays more difficult for your child. In other words, rather than role-playing "perfect" scenarios, your child will be challenged with situations where the outcome is less than desirable, and where he or she will have to cope with rising levels of anxiety.

Review of the Past Week

The therapist will review your child's progress in conducting the previously assigned STIC tasks. In particular, the therapist will look for any signs of avoidance, escape, or otherwise inappropriate management of these situations. If your child did not complete any of the assigned tasks, the therapist will ask your child to recall and discuss the thoughts that were going through his or her mind. Using the STOP procedure, the therapist will help your child examine which "thinking traps" may have interfered with carrying out the STIC task.

If your child did not complete any of the assigned STIC tasks, the therapist will help your child process his or her avoidance of the tasks. The therapist will continue to help your child challenge the negative thoughts that prevent him or her from confronting the avoidance. The therapist will review the dispute handles used to question your child's thoughts, and your child will practice challenging and changing negative thoughts. If your child has completed the STIC assignments, the therapist will examine any difficulties, successes, or other issues with the goal of reinforcing compliance with the homework. In doing so, the therapist will focus your child on what it feels like to actually complete the STIC task, what actually happened, and how your child coped with the situation.

Stepping Up the Behavioral Exposures

The therapist and your child will continue to focus on practicing entering anxiety-provoking situations. New and more challenging items from your child's AAH will be constructed in these sessions. The therapist will begin to present your child with more difficult situations as appropriate. For example, on Mark's AAH (see Figure 5.2), item 6 is "Giving an oral report" in front of the class. The therapist is likely to uncover a variety of negative thoughts for this situation. For example:

> What if I stutter?
>
> What if someone starts laughing at me?
>
> I may not know what to say.
>
> Suppose I can't read a word?
>
> Suppose I mispronounce a word? I'll look stupid.

For this behavioral exposure, the therapist will want Mark to give an oral report and actually experience some of these things that are provoking his anxiety. The purpose of practicing a less-than-perfect job, or having a situation go wrong in some way, is to help your child tolerate undesirable consequences. After all, no one can control what other people think or do, or always be in control of everything. Anyone may stutter, shake, mispronounce a word, or forget or lose his or her place during an oral report. Through practice, your child will learn that situations are usually less than perfect, and that it is normal for situations to go this way.

For Mark's behavioral exposure, the therapist will likely set up the following situations to challenge his negative thoughts and provide him with experience in coping:

1. What if I stutter? What if someone starts laughing at me?

   Mark will be asked to give an oral report in front of the therapist and possibly some assistants. During his report, he will be prompted by the therapist to stutter several times. Each time, an assistant will laugh, look away, roll his or her eyes, lean over and talk to another person, or react in a similar way each time he stutters. Mark's goal for this situation will be to continue to give his report, no matter what the audience does. Following the exposure, the therapist will help Mark process the exposure in various ways, focusing on how anxious he felt and how he actually performed; how bad the outcomes really were; what other possibilities could account for the audience behavior (e.g., people were laughing at something they read; they were tired; they weren't being nice).

2. I may not know what to say. Suppose I can't read a word? Suppose I mispronounce a word?

   During another practice, Mark will be given a report to read that contains difficult words (probably technical or scientific words). The goal of this exposure will be to have Mark actually be unable to pronounce some words. The audience will initially pay attention and listen to the talk. However, as the exposure continues, the audience will act disinterested, snicker, or otherwise behave as though they are not following Mark's talk. The therapist will help Mark cope with and master this situation.

Processing the More Challenging Exposures

The therapist will spend considerable time with your child examining the thoughts and behaviors that occurred during these behavioral exposures. Many children quickly come to understand that it is normal to make mistakes, be embarrassed or uncomfortable, or for other people to be less than nice. These children recognize that their discomfort is momentary and that, in spite of being anxious or slightly embarrassed, in the long run they will be fine. However, some children can be hard on themselves. These children push for situations to turn out perfectly, and it is much more difficult for them to tolerate anything less than perfect. They are anxious about embarrassment, rejection, or humiliation, and their overriding thought is *No one will like me or want to be around me.*

To process the exposure, the therapist will take your child through the scenario step-by-step. At each point, the therapist will analyze your child's thoughts, anxiety ratings, and actual performance behaviors. For example, imagine an exposure where a young girl is to start and carry on a conversation with a peer. The child reports feeling anxious because *I may not know what to say. She may not like me. What if I say something stupid?* During this exposure, the child meets all of her goals: She introduces herself, asks three questions, maintains eye contact, and smiles. However, her anxiety ratings remain high throughout the exposure. This indicates continued high anxiety. Following this exposure, the therapist may process the situation as follows:

T: Okay Stacy, look at your goals. Seems that you met every one. In fact, instead of asking three questions, you actually asked five. What do you think about that?

C: Well, I guess I did okay on that. But I just didn't feel good.

T: What were you thinking about while you were doing this practice?

C: I just kept thinking I was messing up. I thought I looked stupid.

T: Take a look at these goals. How did you mess up? What did you do that was so bad?

C: I don't know. I thought I wasn't talking enough.

T: But you actually asked more questions than you had hoped. And, I also counted that you answered all five of the questions that were asked of you.

C: I did? I didn't realize that.

T: The point here is that, even though you felt nervous, you were doing fine. You were asking and answering questions, and having a real conversation. Can you see that?

C: I kept telling myself that I wasn't doing well.

T: A-ha! So even though you were doing everything you wanted to, you kept those negative thoughts coming. Do you realize what kind of negative thought that is?

C: Canceling out the positive. Even though I was doing okay, I was telling myself I was doing bad.

T: That's it. You've got to let yourself focus on what you're doing, and feel better about that. Let's try it again.

- The therapist will ask your child to practice in real-life the situation role-played during this session. Your child will be required to practice at least three times prior to the next session. Your child will also be asked to record an anxiety rating immediately prior to, and immediately after, this exercise. Talk with your child after each practice, much like the therapist would during session, and focus your child on what really occurred during the practice and what happened to the anxiety. Offer praise and encouragement for attempting and/or completing each practice.
- Continue to implement the normal school-day routine and adhere to it as closely as possible. During the day, your child should do schoolwork and read school-related books when at home.
- Continue to complete the daily logbooks, noting any specific issues or situations that arise during the week.

Sessions 5–6: Advanced Maturing of Treatment

Sessions 5–6 will involve helping your child progress through the main portion of his or her AAH. Through role-playing and new real-life exposures, the therapist will help your child enter and stay in those social and/or evaluative situations that he or she is anxious about and avoids. A major focus of these exposures will be to elicit your child's negative self-talk and help your child challenge and change these thoughts. In these sessions, your child will continue to practice changing thoughts to a coping focus. The therapist will spend time role-playing and modeling the process of cognitive restructuring (changing thoughts). You may be invited to attend these sessions, to observe the therapist, and become better at coaching your child in using these cognitive strategies. The degree of your involvement will likely depend on a combination of factors, including the severity of your child's school refusal problem, his or her age and developmental level, and any special needs that he or she may have. Moreover, if your child's motivation is not strong, the therapist may enlist your help in finding appropriate incentives to reward your child for doing the therapy work.

Because your child has been refusing school due to anxiety in social and/or evaluative situations, it will be necessary to involve other people if the treatment is to be successful. For example, you may have your child's peers come to your home for a play date. This will give your child an opportunity to practice conversation and related social skills. For the most part, other children or adults do not need to know that your child is testing his or her new coping skills or working on a personal problem. However, you may need to inform your child's teacher about certain exposures or situations that your child will be facing. Examples include speaking up more in class or asking the teacher for help.

If your child has been shy or quiet, it is possible that other people have come to expect less interaction with him or her. Therefore, the therapist will inform you what to tell the teacher to facilitate your child's progress in trying new social behaviors. Also, your child will need to be gradually exposed to various social and/or evaluative situations outside of school. If you have been speaking for your child in public places, such as restaurants or stores, the therapist will help you step back and coach your child to speak for himself or herself. It is not unusual for parents of adolescents with social or evaluative anxiety to comment on things that their son or daughter is *not* doing that are typical of teenage behavior (e.g., ordering food in a restaurant, answering or talking on the telephone, paying for their own purchases at the mall). The involvement of other people and a variety of social situations will be the focus of your child's STIC tasks throughout the remainder of treatment.

Realistic Thinking

The therapist will begin each session discussing your child's progress in following through with the weekly STIC tasks. This will allow the therapist to evaluate your child's ability to identify and challenge negative thoughts. As your child's skill in using cognitive restructuring improves, he or she will develop greater tolerance for approaching and staying in challenging social and/or evaluative situations.

The popular press and pop psychology movement once promoted the concept of "positive thinking" as a way to overcome negative and distressing emotions. Positive thinking entails repeating thoughts to oneself such as *I can do this, I'm smart,* and *I'm a good person,* to neutralize negative thoughts. Research and clinical experience explain why some people never get better through the use of positive thinking. Positive thinking has been shown to actually interfere with focusing on and accomplishing a task. In fact, children who are test anxious actually do just as poorly or worse when given positive statements such as *I'm smart, I can do this.* Positive thoughts don't provide any real information or coping solutions for the child to rely on and use in a given situation. During a test, for example, a child can become so focused on trying to convince himself or herself that *I am smart,* that concentration on the actual task is disrupted. As the child recognizes that he or she is not completing the task, his or her levels of frustration and physical tension increase. This sets into motion the cycle of disruptive physical sensations, thoughts, and behaviors, each reinforcing the other and making the situation worse. In this case, saying *I am smart* leads to sensations such as muscle tension or headache, disruption in completing the task, and the resultant *Oh no, I can't do this after all!* that further perpetuates the child's tension, negative thoughts, and poor performance.

In contrast to positive thinking, research demonstrates that healthy thinking is the predominant style of thought used by well-adjusted individuals. Healthy thinking is characterized by realistically examining a situation and the resources available to manage it. Healthy thinking is reality-based, focused on problem-solving and task management, and characterized by adaptive thoughts. By this point in your child's program, the therapist has helped your child use the STOP program or similar cognitive restructuring techniques to uncover irrational or negative beliefs (The **S** and **T** steps). Your child has practiced changing these negative thoughts to more realistic and adaptive coping statements (the **O** step that involves the use of dispute handles). Role-plays and behavioral exposures have given your child opportunities to test his or her thoughts and gather evidence that he or she can cope with anxious situations. Continued exposure to challenging situations will give your child evidence to refute and change negative thinking.

Trials of Childhood: Examples of Social/Evaluative Exposures and Restructuring

Children and adolescents with social anxiety may be anxious about a wide range of situations involving other people, tests, oral presentations, or sports or musical performances. If your child's social anxiety is focused on only one type of social situation, it is considered non-generalized. This is the case with individuals who are otherwise fine but become extremely anxious when having to give a talk in front of others. Many children and adolescents, however, are anxious about many social situations. This is called generalized social anxiety. It is normal for social anxiety to increase as children enter adolescence. However, for children more prone to experiencing generalized social anxiety, adolescence can be an even more difficult and distressing stage of life. The therapist will construct more challenging exposures during this phase of treatment so that your child will be encouraged to use his or her cognitive restructuring skills more readily. Preparation for each exposure is the same: your child defines several concrete goals, identifies his or her negative or automatic thoughts, and provides a rational alternative thought for each, using dispute handles. Following each exposure, the therapist will help your child develop a healthy thinking style. The following are examples of exposures and cognitive restructuring procedures for different social anxieties.

Example 1: Tackling Test Anxiety

In exposures conducted for test anxiety, the therapist will administer tests and quizzes to your child. The therapist may request sample tests from your child's teacher or develop tests based on your child's current schoolwork. The exposure will manipulate a number of situations that your child is likely to encounter, such as being timed, having multiple-choice or essay questions, and being surprised with a pop quiz in therapy as opposed to a planned quiz. A typical post-exposure processing follows:

T: Okay, so what happened during this test?

C: I got only eight out of ten. I knew I'd bomb that test.

T: You do well in math, tell me the percentage that you got on this quiz.

C: Eighty. I only got an eighty.

T: What's the worst thing that could happen with an eighty on a test?

C: I could fail math, and then I'd fail my other subjects too.

T: Let's take one thing at a time. Tell me, is eighty percent a failure?

C: No, but it's only a B.

T: Wow, what kind of thought is that, "it's only a B"?

C: (Looks at list of thought labels.) Oh, I just disqualified a positive. Okay, I did better than a C.

T: So, rephrase that thought. What is really going on with a B?

C: Okay, I got a B, and that's a passing grade.

T: Okay, and tell me, have you ever failed a test before?

C: No, but I got a C once.

T: And?

C: A C is still passing.

T: Okay, so have you ever failed a subject before because you got a C or a B?

C: No.

T: So, how likely is it that you would fail the test and then fail the subject?

C: Well, it could happen.

T: Do you study for your tests?

C: Yes.

T: What else do you do to prepare for your tests?

C: I do my homework.

T: Okay, so tell me realistically, how likely is it that you would fail the test and then fail the subject?

C: Okay, it's not really likely that I'd fail the test.

T: Why? What is the evidence that you wouldn't fail? Put it all together.

C: It's not likely I'd fail, because I do study and I do all my homework.

T: Give me a percentage for how likely it is from 0 to 100 percent.

C: Well, it's really only maybe a 5% chance.

T: What's really the worst thing that could happen?

C: I could get a B in the class, but that's not failing.

The therapist will give repeated test simulations to your child, each followed by the cognitive restructuring steps outlined in STOP. The therapist will emphasize examining the evidence for your child's anxiety and looking realistically at potential outcomes and their consequences. Some children are anxious about tests because of learning disabilities or because they do not do well on tests. The focus of this treatment is on managing anxiety that can develop due to a history of poor performance. In cases of true learning problems, a therapist may coordinate treatment with a tutor or special education teacher so the child with special needs can manage anxiety and then benefit most from appropriate academic services available to him or her.

Example 2: Standing up to Shyness

Some shy or quiet children who worry about what other people think of them may be at risk for developing clinical levels of social and/or evaluative anxiety. Shyness is generally accepted in our culture as a normal variant of personality. By itself, it is not a problem. However, for the child who shrinks away from making friends, is unable to speak up for his or her own needs, or is otherwise unable to warm up to people, shyness is so extreme that it is problematic. It is also unfortunate that shy or quiet children are often overlooked as teachers struggle to teach in overcrowded classrooms. Children with extreme shyness often suffer with overwhelming anxiety before others recognize the need to help them. The focus of a shy child's exposures will not be to remake that child's personality. This is important to understand: your child will not become someone he or she doesn't want to be. There will be no radical change in your child's temperament or personality. Instead, by addressing social anxiety in treatment, your child will be more relaxed in social situations. Your child will be able to make decisions about what he or she wants to do based on his or her preferences instead of on anxiety about rejection, embarrassment, or feelings of incompetence.

Exposures for shy children and adolescents will involve interactions with different people in different situations, such as starting conversations in the cafeteria; calling a classmate for missed homework; asking a question in class; joining a group of kids who are already playing together; asking someone to stop doing something annoying; saying "No" when desired. In the following example, the therapist helps the child question the evidence for his or her anxiety about what other people think.

T: What is the hardest thing about school for you?

C: I guess the other kids.

T: What is it about the other kids that bothers you?

C: I don't know. I don't think they really like me.

T: Why do you think that, Tami? What happens with the other kids?

C: No one really talks to me. I don't have any friends and I don't have anyone to sit with in the cafeteria or at recess.

T: Have you ever tried to talk to the other kids?

C: Yes.

T: When was the last time that you tried?

C: I don't know . . . it was a while ago. Maybe last year.

T: Well Tami, then it sounds like you've given up trying to talk to others.

C: It's no use. I'm afraid of them not liking me. I know already they don't like me.

T: Wait, let's look at what's really going on. You may have tried last year. But this year you haven't tried at all, have you?

C: No.

T: What are some of the reasons why the other kids don't talk to you?

C: Because they don't like me, I told you that. They all know each other and they're all friends.

T: Okay, first tell me what kind of a thought is "Because they don't like me"?

C: It's mind reading, or maybe fortune telling. I know I'm predicting that they don't like me, but I really can't know what they think.

T: That's right! What evidence do you have, besides the fact that no one has tried to talk to you recently, that they don't like you?

C: Well, none really.

T: So, what other reasons may there be for the kids not talking to you?

C: I don't know, I guess because I don't try to talk to them.

T: Maybe. Where do you usually hang out during lunch or recess?

C: I just stay in the classroom, or go to the library.

T: So, is it fair to say that you don't even go near the other kids?

C: Yeah.

T: So, what evidence is there that they don't like you?

C: None.

T: And what else may be going on?

C: Maybe because I don't hang around the other kids, and don't go talk to them, that's why they don't talk to me. But it's so hard! What if I don't know what to say?

T: Okay, right. One thing at a time. Remember, slow down that tape of automatic thoughts in your mind, and dispute one thought at a time. Maybe the other kids don't talk to you because you're not hanging around the cafeteria or recess area. Maybe they don't have a chance to talk with you.

C: Yeah, I can see that.

T: Okay, and, because you haven't done this in a while, it'll be hard. Trying to talk with someone is hard if you're out of practice. But, you also said "What if I don't know what to say?"

C: Yeah, then there will be some stupid silence, and I'll look like a jerk.

T: Oh, but if the other kid doesn't talk, will she look stupid?

C: What? No . . .

T: So, why would you look stupid if you were quiet for a moment? Let me ask you something. How many people does it take to have a conversation?

C: I guess at least two.

T: Yes. So, in a conversation with two people, and you being one of them, how much of the conversation are you responsible for?

C: Um, just half of it.

T: That's right. You're only responsible for fifty percent of the conversation. The other person is also responsible. So, if there's silence, it's not just because of you, but also because of the other person. Right?

C: Yeah, that's right.

T: So, what can you do to prepare yourself to start a conversation with someone?

C: Well, I guess I'm only responsible for half of the conversation. And, if I haven't talked with this person, it may be hard at first. I guess I have to try it, and make myself hang around where the other kids are.

T: Good going.

Shy children need repeated experience with conversations and being around other people. The therapist will focus on increasing your child's ability to physically place himself or herself closer to peers, as well as on improving conversational and social skills. The therapist will continuously challenge your child's dysfunctional attitudes and beliefs as your child gathers new information about social situations and about being the focus of attention.

Example 3: Overcoming Gym Jitters

Performance-based classes or activities are likely to cause jitters in many children and adults. A child who experiences social anxiety, however, may be even more anxious about performance-based activities and may develop an inappropriate strategy of avoidance to manage the problem. If you have noticed your child complaining of stomachaches or illness on gym days, or if his or her guitar suddenly snaps all its strings right before the annual recital, you may suspect high levels of social anxiety. Children who refuse to attend school due to performance-based anxiety will try to avoid these situations at all costs. Or, they may endure a situation while under great distress, and then drop out of the activity at their first chance. The following dialogue illustrates the main concerns of a child who refused to attend school due to performance anxiety.

C: Going to gym was the main problem. I just couldn't stand it when everyone laughed at me. I can't do sports. And I was always picked last for everything. It stinks.

T: Tell me more about gym class. I want to know who's in your class and the activities that you have to do.

C: All the guys from my homeroom are there. They're all jocks, every one of them. We started out doing basketball. What a joke. I never played before. Then we had to play football. I was so bad in basketball that no one picked me for football. The coach had to put me on a team.

T: Let's break this down. All the guys in your gym class were jocks? That means that every single one of them played on a team sport at your school?

C: No, not every one. Most of them.

T: How many kids are in that class, and how many are on teams?

C: All right, so there's 20 guys in the class, and maybe six play on the school teams. But that's a lot.

T: Okay, and of those 14 guys who were not on the teams, they were all total jocks too. Is that what you're telling me?

C: No. My friend Brian wasn't too good at anything either. But everyone likes him. He got picked before I did for the teams.

T: So, Joey, tell me this, when you go to gym, what do you do? When you first get to gym class, what are you likely to do?

C: So no one will talk to me. So maybe they'll forget about me and I won't have to play the sport.

T: Then, is it possible that the other guys pick you last because you're sitting on the side, reading or trying to not be noticed?

C: Yeah, it's possible.

T: And, is it possible that if you tried to hang around a little more, that the other guys might start picking you sooner?

C: Sure, anything is possible.

T: Let me ask you this. You don't like all sports, right?

C: No, I like to play tennis. I just don't like basketball and football.

T: Oh. Do you get to play tennis in gym class?

C: Yeah, but not until the spring, and only for three weeks.

T: Oh. And are these jocks good at tennis, too?

C: No, especially the bigger guys.

T: So, is it fair to say that not everyone can be good at everything?

C: Yeah.

T: And when those big jocks mess up on the tennis court, does anyone tease them?

C: Yeah, their friends laugh about it.

T: Okay. So, let's sum this up. Not everyone has a great body, but other kids still change together. And, not everyone is good at everything, and even the jocks get teased. And, if you sit by yourself with reading, you may be overlooked by the others, but not excluded on purpose. Right?

In this example, the therapist uncovered faulty beliefs and helped the child examine what he could do. Joey did play tennis, but he discounted this fact and focused on his misery in the moment. Joey also compared himself to the jocks, and not all the other children, thus making himself feel all the more different and awkward. The therapist will help your child change "all or none" thinking to more realistic appraisals of the situation and his or her abilities. In vivo exposures for Joey would involve leaving his book (a safety signal) behind and going up to the boys he is familiar with during gym class.

Children in this situation may benefit from some basic social skills training in making and keeping eye contact, starting and joining conversations, and being assertive. If your child is teased in a mean way, the therapist will train him or her to ignore teasing and not respond to the teasers. This is accomplished through teasing exposures, where the therapist role-plays with your child. The therapist teaches your child to focus on what he or she is doing, to take deep diaphragmatic breaths, and to refrain from giving any attention to the teasers. In such situations, teasers usually quit if they are not reinforced. If your child is bullied or touched physically by a teaser, the therapist instructs him or her to report this to an adult who will listen and who has authority over the other children (e.g., coach, principal). Most often, children who are teased attempt to tease back. Some are able to do this successfully and the teasing either becomes good-natured or stops altogether. Other children are unable to tease or fight back verbally, and by trying to do so they draw more negative attention to themselves. That is why it is preferable to train children not to respond to the provocation.

Homework

Homework assignments after sessions 5–6 may include the following:

- Your child will be given in vivo exposure (STIC) tasks to complete between sessions, along with appropriate cognitive restructuring exercises for each task. Remember to coach your child through these tasks according to the guidance from the therapist. The dialogues in Chapters 4–5 give you practical examples for coaching your child to examine the realistic evidence for his or her faulty beliefs.
- Practice STIC tasks assigned for school-related situations. Your child should be attending at least part of the school day by the end of sessions 5–6. These STIC tasks will increasingly involve your child interacting with both children and adults; be sure to help your child follow through with these exposures. This may require some adjustment on your part. If you are used to a child who has a quiet schedule or does not invite other children to your house, this will temporarily change. It is important to schedule your time so that you can get your child to school or to social situations involving different people. Although it may seem excessive to have your child attend some type of social outing three or more times a week, the frequency of these outings will be cut back to a normal level during later treatment.
- Continue to complete the daily logbooks, noting any specific issues or situations that arise during the week.

Sessions 7–8: Completing Treatment

By this point in your child's treatment, he or she will be expected to attend school on a full-time basis. The therapist may have helped your child return to school by actually going in with him or her the first few times. These assisted exposures will be invaluable when your child confronts an anxiety-provoking situation in real life. The purpose of the STIC tasks has been to prepare your child for confrontations and to give him or her practice in managing emotions during these times. Most importantly, the STIC tasks have been designed to gradually bring your child to full-time school attendance and tapered support from the therapist. He or she should be taking most of the responsibility for the treatment process and applying what was learned in real-life situations. If necessary, the therapist will continue to implement techniques from previous sessions to help your child achieve this goal.

Tell the therapist if you use different punishments for your children. For example, you may punish your child with school refusal behavior much more than your other children. In addition, the therapist may ask you to describe whether each punishment was effective and whether you still use it. Identify your uses of each punishment over the past few days and how your child responded.

The therapist will also want to know how you used these punishments in the past few weeks or months. For example, have you tried time-out? If so, what procedures did you use? How long did you try it? Did both parents implement time-out? Did your child know the house rules before being placed in time-out? Have you tried grounding? If so, did your child leave the house anyway? Did he or she tear up the bedroom? Did he or she say "I don't care"? All past punishments must be discussed in depth. The therapist will also want to know how effective you think punishment will be in changing your child's current behavior. The therapist may discuss with you some possible new rules and punishments and get your feedback. Be sure to give your input.

Setting Up Rewards for School Attendance

The therapist will ask you to list rewards you have given in the past few days for your child's good behavior. Examples include verbal praise, attention, extra play or reading time with your child, food, toys, money, or an easing of responsibilities, among others. Let the therapist know if these rewards differ from child to child. As with punishments, the therapist will ask you to describe whether each reward was effective and whether you still use it.

The therapist will also explore how you used rewards in the past few weeks or months. For example, what system of reward did you set up for your child? The therapist will want to know how effective you think rewards will be in changing your child's current behavior. In doing so, the therapist may suggest some new rewards. Be sure to give your input. Finally, the therapist will talk to you about your time and other resources that may affect what rewards and punishments can be used in treatment.

Homework

Homework assignments after session 1 may include the following:

- Keep a list of the commands you give to each child between this session and the next one. Write the command in the exact wording you used.
- Keep a daily record of your family's morning routine between this session and the next one.
- Think about changes in your morning routine that may help your child go to school.
- Think about other punishments and rewards you have used in the past and possible new ones that you could use in the future.

- Try to adhere to a regular school-day schedule, even if only in the morning prior to school. This includes early wakening, dressing, and preparing for school as if going, and completing school assignments.
- Continue to complete the daily logbooks, noting any specific issues or situations that arise during the week.

Session 2: Intensifying Treatment

This section describes how a therapist may intensify treatment for a child refusing school for attention. Again, the major focus is you and your spouse and the major goal of treatment is to shift attention away from school refusal behaviors and toward school attendance. This will involve changing your commands, setting up daily routines, setting up punishments for school refusal behavior, and setting up rewards for school attendance.

Changing Parent Commands

The therapist may begin this session by reviewing the list of commands you gave to your children over the past few days. The therapist will pay particular attention to commands you gave your child who is refusing school. In the following example, **T** represents the therapist, **F** represents the child's father, and **M** represents the child's mother:

T: I see that one command you gave yesterday was "Clean your room." Can you tell me about that?

F: I told him he should clean his room. He didn't get around to it, of course.

T: When you told him to clean his room, what was he doing at the time?

F: Watching television. He always seems to find something to do when we ask him to do something.

T: I see that another command you gave was more urgent and about school.

M: Yes, I asked him this morning to stop hanging on to me.

T: What does "hanging on" mean?

M: He was all over me, whining and complaining about having to go to school. He didn't want to go and was bugging me to let him stay home.

T: Okay, you say that he was all over you—what exactly does that mean?

M: Well, it's hard to describe. He comes over to me, sometimes grabs my leg or lies at my feet when I'm trying to do something, like make the kids' lunches.

The therapist will begin to change some of the statements you make to your child. He or she will check your list of commands for errors. Listen carefully and be open to what he or she suggests. The therapist may point out specific ways to make your commands more effective. For example:

- Say exactly when the command is to be carried out. In the example dialogue, no timelines were set for starting the task. When you give a command, give a time limit. Give a five-minute limit for starting chores such as cleaning a room or washing dishes. If the command needs to be carried out more immediately, as was the case with the mother's command, then give a 10-second limit. The therapist will help you decide which commands need to be obeyed within the 10-second limit. These will be many of the commands you give when trying to get your child to school.
- Say exactly what you require of your child and keep it simple. The command "Clean your room," for example, has different possible meanings. Does this include dusting, vacuuming, making the bed, and straightening the dresser? Does it mean more than that? Instead of this vague command, try something more specific such as "Pick up your clothes from the bedroom floor and hang them up on hangers in the closet. Start within five minutes." Instead of "Stop hanging on to me," try "Take your hands off of me. You have 10 seconds."
- Be sure that your child is physically capable of carrying out the command. For example, if your 5-year-old can't hang up clothes in the closet, don't ask him or her to do it. Your child should also be able to understand all parts of the command. Stick with simple one-step commands first. Ask your child to repeat the command if necessary to be sure he or she understands it.
- Be sure that nothing competes with your child's attention (e.g., watching television, talking with friends) when giving a command. Although some children are capable of "not hearing" or "forgetting" a command, make sure that there is no possibility of this. In particular, make direct eye contact with your child when you give a command.
- Be sure the command is a command and not an option or question. In the example, the father indicated that the child "should" clean his room. In addition, the mother "asked" her son to "stop hanging on to me." These words suggest that the child has a choice. Eliminate this choice by giving short, direct commands in sentence form.

- Eliminate sarcastic criticism of your child. Sarcasm is often noted by children, who may think that they will get no reinforcement even when they do comply. Stay neutral in your tone when you give a command. This neutrality will be especially important later when dealing with your attention-seeking child.
- Cut down on extra speech during a command (e.g., don't give lectures) and be sure you do not reward your child by having someone else carry out the command (e.g., having a sibling do the dishes) for him or her.
- Engage in a task with your child after giving a command (e.g., pick up toys in a room with your child; prepare for work as the child prepares for school).
- Always provide some reward for obeying a command (compliance) and some punishment for failing to obey a command (noncompliance).

The therapist will go through all the commands on your list and help you change them as necessary. Try to come up with good changes yourself so you can learn to build effective commands on your own. Focus especially on commands you give in the morning for school attendance. In addition, if excessive reassurance-seeking by your child is a problem now, talk to the therapist about the possibility of starting procedures to address this behavior.

Setting Up Regular Routines

The therapist will also review your description of a typical school-day morning in your house. He or she will pay special attention to the times the children rise from bed, wash and get dressed, eat, brush their teeth, do extra activities such as watch television, prepare for school, and leave the house to go to school. In addition, the therapist will review *your* typical routine during the morning, including your behaviors toward your children.

The therapist will then give you feedback about changes that are necessary to regulate your morning routine and improve your responses to your children. Be open to these changes and give your input. For example, the therapist may want you to set up a stricter morning routine. He or she may recommend that you have your child rise from bed about 90–120 minutes before school starts. Do this even if your child is not currently attending school. Allow your child only 10 minutes between waking up and rising from bed.

In addition, the therapist will help you set times for your other morning activities. Your schedule should be flexible but strict enough to allow for a smooth transition to school. The following schedule may be used as a rough guide:

6:50 a.m.	Wake your child (require him or her to be out of bed by 7:00 a.m.).
7:00–7:20 a.m.	Child goes to the bathroom and washes as necessary.
7:20–7:40 a.m.	Child dresses and accessorizes as necessary.

7:40–8:00 a.m.	Child eats breakfast and discusses his or her day with parents.
8:00–8:20 a.m.	Child makes final preparations for school (e.g., books, jacket).
8:20–8:35 a.m.	Child goes to school with parents (or rides the bus).
8:40 a.m.	Child enters school and classroom.

Setting Up Punishments for School Refusal Behavior

The therapist will review the list of punishments you used in the past to discipline your children, looking specifically at the effectiveness of each and how it was used. You will discuss your attitudes toward each punishment as well. Be sure to discuss any new rules or punishments that you think are important. The therapist will probably want to focus on five specific school refusal behaviors. These can be chosen from information gathered during assessment, and you should rate them from most problematic to least problematic. For example:

1. Refusal to move (most problematic)
2. Aggression/hitting one's sister or parent
3. Crying
4. Excessive reassurance-seeking (asking the same question more than twice in one hour)
5. Screaming (least problematic).

The therapist will then ask you to choose a specific punishment that you could use for your child's two least problematic behaviors. It is important at this point to focus on less problematic behaviors. That way, you can practice what to do with less effort and experience some success with the process. However, if you feel comfortable addressing more of your child's behaviors at this time, let the therapist know. Punishments may also be set for noncompliance to commands.

The punishment should be practical and be given both in the morning and after school. Your child should know that school refusal behavior is serious and will be addressed at all times of the day, not just in the morning. Examples of punishment for an attention-seeking child include ignoring, time-out, working through misbehavior without extra attention, and going to bed early. In some cases, however, stronger or more tangible punishments are needed.

In addition, the therapist will go over all possible scenarios that could occur in the next few mornings and form a plan with you to deal with them. Although this may take some time, knowing how to respond to any behavior is important for putting you in charge of your home life. As much as possible, work toward the goal of getting your child to school.

Note that some children will behave worse to get their parents to give in. This is known as an "extinction burst" and can damage the therapy process. If your child forces you to give up now, then he or she will misbehave even more later when you try to assert yourself again. Be aware of this possibility and try hard to follow through on commands and punishments. Be sure you know exactly what to do during the next few mornings when trying to get your child to school. In addition, stay in regular contact with the therapist during the next few days.

Setting Up Rewards for School Attendance

The therapist will also review the list of rewards you used in the past for good behavior. He or she will review the effectiveness and desirability of each reward, as well as your attitudes about each and how you used them in the past. Talk about new rewards you think are important.

The therapist will first ask you to choose a reward for two good behaviors. Try to make the reward attention-based. For example, if your child does not scream or ask a question multiple times, then give a lot of verbal praise in the morning and schedule a time at night when you and your child can do something together (e.g., read, play a game). In some cases, however, stronger or more tangible rewards are needed.

The therapist will instruct your child about the expected routine, appropriate behaviors, and punishments and rewards. Your child will be reminded that it is his or her behavior that determines whether you give punishments or rewards. You should, after the therapist, repeat this to your child in session and at home to reinforce your role in taking charge.

Homework

Homework assignments after session 2 may include the following:

- Continue to keep a list of commands you give to each child. Change your commands according to the session 2 discussion. If you have a spouse, meet with him or her each night to discuss changes you should make for the next day.
- Beginning with the next school day after this session, wake your child 90–120 minutes before school starts and implement the normal school-day routine. Follow this routine as closely as possible. During the day, your child should do schoolwork and read school-related books when at home.
- Use the punishments for the two behaviors you have chosen.
- Use the rewards for the absence of the two behaviors you have chosen.
- Contact the therapist if any problems arise.
- Continue to complete the daily logbooks, noting any specific issues or situations that arise during the week.

Sessions 3–4: Maturing of Treatment

This section describes the "maturing" of treatment of children who refuse school for attention by revisiting procedures from sessions 1–2. At this point in treating your child, the therapist will help you focus more on your morning and evening routines and on changing your child's school refusal behaviors. This may include ignoring inappropriate behaviors, physically taking your child to school, and dealing with your child during the daytime if he or she stays home following misbehaviors. Hopefully, you will begin to see less school refusal behavior and learn important skills that will help you solve other problems in the future. In addition, many parents learn skills in therapy that are helpful in dealing with their other children.

Changing Parent Commands

The therapist will review the list of commands you give to your children. The therapist will check for problems in these commands and give you constructive feedback. Be open to this feedback. The therapist will also ask you about nonverbal gestures and parent disagreements that could hurt the effectiveness of your commands. For example, some parents give commands without firmness of tone or eye contact, and other parents may undercut their spouses by inadvertently or deliberately giving in to a child. The therapist will want you to address these problems immediately.

The therapist will focus on recent commands you have given to your child with school refusal behavior, and those you have given in the morning before school. The therapist will review each command and note important things that you are *not* saying or doing. For example:

T: It seems that you had two good days and two bad days this week since the last session. Can you tell me what the major difference was between these two sets of days?

M: On Monday and Wednesday, John (child's father) and I seemed really to be in "sync." We were working together to get the kids up and going to school, and we backed each other up as we talked about last time. (To husband:) Don't you think so?

F: Yeah, I do, I guess it broke down a bit on the other days.

T: Let's talk about that. What exactly "broke down"?

F: There was a lot more resistance to going to school on both those days, and he (the child) had a lot of tantrums. We started yelling and nothing much got accomplished. I had to go to work, and I guess he wore her (child's mother) down.

In this sample case, a therapist would explore what led to the breakdown of the treatment procedures. The most likely reasons for breakdown include parent disagreements, one parent leaving the situation, and increased child misbehaviors. When these things happen, parents are more likely to give unclear commands (e.g., *Will you please be quiet?* and *I just wish you would go to school*). You and the therapist should find out what is breaking down your commands and correct any problems as soon as possible. It may be necessary to change your work schedules or ask other people to help you bring your child to school.

If your child has clearly increased his or her misbehavior to force you to abandon your commands or to give up on the set routines and rewards and punishments, be sure to tell the therapist. He or she will help you develop ways of working through your child's behavior problem to accomplish your goals. To back up your commands, for example, you may have to physically dress your child and bring him or her downstairs while he or she is throwing a tantrum or is becoming "dead" weight. By session 4, you should know what makes a good command. If you are uncertain or if extenuating circumstances (e.g., spouse leaving home early) continue to interfere with your commands, talk to the therapist.

The therapist may raise the issue of ignoring inappropriate behaviors. Many parents adjust to a child who is always demanding attention by simply responding to the child whenever he or she acts up. For example, some parents have a tendency, over time, to leave a child alone when he or she is playing quietly (*Don't disturb him*), but to react immediately when he or she is disruptive (*Stop that now*). As the child grows older, however, he or she learns that the best way to get parental attention is to misbehave.

Among children who refuse school, a common way of getting attention is to exaggerate physical complaints. This applies especially to vague complaints like headaches, stomachaches, and nausea. Attention-seeking children rarely complain of specific, identifiable symptoms like fever or vomiting (although it is possible). If you and the therapist are sure that your child is exaggerating physical symptoms for attention and not because of a medical condition, then you may want to ignore these complaints. However, you should first rule out any possible medical conditions.

To ignore exaggerated physical complaints, the therapist may ask you to do different things in the morning. Examples include stopping eye contact with your child (i.e., looking away when he or she complains), using time-out, working through tantrums or excess verbal behavior, paying attention to well-behaved siblings, and talking to your spouse. When engaging in these behaviors, be sure that your child does not play one parent against the other to get what he or she wants. In two-parent families, is not uncommon for one parent to ignore a child's inappropriate behavior only to have the other parent attend to it. Consistency between you and your spouse is extremely important to present a united front to your child. Your child must learn that misbehavior, including exaggerated physical complaints, will not be tolerated by anyone. Conversely, be sure to praise and otherwise reward your child when he or she is not complaining of exaggerated symptoms.

Ignoring some of your child's behavior, especially complaints of physical symptoms, will be hard. Some parents feel guilty about being overly stern with their child. Some are concerned that something might actually be wrong with their child, or that they will cause long-term psychological harm to their child. Some worry that their child will no longer trust them with personal information. If you do feel guilty or have other concerns about ignoring misbehavior, tell the therapist about it. He or she may give you more information about differences between being firm and being overly strict. The therapist may also refer your child for a medical evaluation to ensure that nothing is actually physically wrong.

Ignoring exaggerated complaints will not cause psychological harm to your child. In fact, as children learn that their parents will attend only to realistic and not to exaggerated complaints, their respect for their parents often grows and they may be more likely to confide in their parents in the future. When you are in doubt about downplaying child misbehaviors or exaggerated physical complaints, remember that the key goals of this treatment are to shift your attention to more positive child behaviors and to put you more in charge of your home life.

Setting Up Regular Routines

The therapist will review the routine you set up with your family and discuss any changes that you made. If you have made changes to the daily routine to make it work better, or want to suggest changes, be sure to tell the therapist. He or she will emphasize structured, consistent routines so that your child becomes used to what is happening (or is going to happen) in the morning. The therapist may work with you on the nighttime routine as well. In general, children should have set times for coming home from school, completing homework, eating dinner, playing, and preparing for bed. The order of these activities may change, of course, depending on your family's situation. In addition, you and the therapist may agree to limit playtime or increase homework time as necessary. If your child is not in school at all, you should obtain schoolwork from the teacher and have your child work on it at home during the day and/or evening.

By session 4, you should know what makes up an efficient routine. If you are uncertain, talk to the therapist. Also, review with the therapist the previous mornings and evenings and indicate what could be improved. Talk about extenuating circumstances that interfered with the routines. Common problems include dawdling siblings, lack of energy, increased child misbehavior, constant changes in work and other schedules, and having other priorities. Talk to the therapist about the advantages and disadvantages of suspending your child's social activities at night and on the weekends (e.g., Scouts, soccer practice, dance lessons) until he or she is attending school full-time.

Forced School Attendance

If your child is not attending school at all or is missing most of school, start thinking about physically bringing him or her into the classroom. For many children who refuse school for attention, forced school attendance is effective. However, it must be used with caution. You should physically take your child to school *only under certain circumstances*. These circumstances include:

- a child refusing school only for attention and without any significant distress or anxiety,
- parents who are willing to take the child to school and school officials who are willing to meet the child at the door of the school building and escort the child to class,
- the presence of two parents or one parent and another adult who can take the child to school,
- a child who understands what will happen if he or she refuses school,
- a child who is currently missing most school days, and
- a child who is under age 11 years.

By session 3, the therapist may raise this issue with you and discuss how the process works. However, if there is some urgency in getting your child back to school, you may pursue forced school attendance now. *Thoroughly discuss this procedure with the therapist before attempting it.* Think about whether you have the energy, ability, and desire to follow through with forced school attendance.

By session 4, start thinking about physically bringing your child into school if the circumstances for using this procedure are met. The first step is to discuss with the therapist how you feel about the procedure. If you feel you are willing and able to put forth the effort that is required, then you may proceed. However, if you have any hesitation or guilt, you should talk to the therapist before moving ahead. Remember that hesitation on your part may be exploited by your child and may make future attempts at school attendance much harder. If you are hesitant, wait before using this procedure or use other techniques recommended by the therapist.

Forced school attendance usually involves some physical contact with the child. In most cases, this means getting the child into the car or into the school building. Most children stop their attention-getting behavior once in school, so forced school attendance usually refers to morning behaviors that are the parents' responsibility. In most cases, the necessary physical force is simply picking the child up and carrying him or her. The treatment described in this workbook does not, of course, sanction any contact that could harm the child.

Forced school attendance typically starts at the end of the morning routine. The parent tells the child to get into the car or bus and to enter the school building once there. If the child does not obey these commands, the parent gives a warning. The warning should be short and clear (e.g., *Go now or we will take you there*). If the child obeys, the parent gives verbal praise. If the child does not obey, the parents should pick the child up and carry him or her into the car or school. School officials should be forewarned and be ready to help. If there are two parents, both should carry the child and ignore or work through the child's tantrums. One parent should drive the car while the other parent sits in the back seat with the child to prevent escape. The parents should stay neutral or "matter-of-fact" in their tone and give the child very little verbal attention.

You should stop forced school attendance if your child is overanxious or if the situation becomes unbearable for you. The danger in stopping, however, is that your child will learn that you will give in if his or her misbehavior is severe enough. *Therefore, forced school attendance must be used only under the right circumstances and with strong follow-through. Be sure to thoroughly discuss forced school attendance with the therapist if you think it is a reasonable option.*

Setting Up Punishments for School Refusal Behavior

The therapist will talk with you about any past or present punishments you have given for school refusal behavior. Discuss how you prefer to discipline your child, your feelings about punishment, and any extenuating circumstances. In addition, the therapist will review your child's school refusal behavior since the last session and how you used punishment. In particular, the therapist will review how you punished the two lowest-severity behaviors.

If you had problems with the punishments since the last session or found they didn't work, the therapist will want to discuss how and what punishments were given. If the punishments had some effect on your child's behavior, then the therapist will ask you to punish the next highest-severity school refusal behavior. Refer to session 2 and your established hierarchy of problematic school refusal behaviors. Go over all relevant scenarios with the therapist and discuss any important issues that you think might come up in the next few days.

By session 4, you should know which punishments are most effective. If you do not, then talk to the therapist. Also, review the previous mornings and evenings and indicate what could be improved. Talk about circumstances (e.g., inconsistency between parents) that interfered with your use of punishment.

Daytime Procedures

At this stage in treatment, if your child is still missing most days of school, then you and the therapist can set up daytime procedures. If your child is missing school during the day, he or she should sit in a chair under your supervision during school hours. You could do this at home or at work if necessary. You should avoid verbal or physical attention beyond what is absolutely necessary. In addition, your child's setting should be as dull as possible. At the end of school hours, you should give the normal punishments (e.g., grounded in room doing homework). If school refusal behavior continues for the majority of the week, then give appropriate punishments for the weekend. Be sure to thoroughly discuss daytime procedures with the therapist if you think that they are a reasonable option.

Setting Up Rewards for School Attendance

Discuss with the therapist any past or present information about rewards for school attendance, including their effectiveness, your feelings about the rewards, and any extenuating circumstances. In particular, the therapist will want to review how successful the rewards were in changing your child's behavior since the previous session. Feel free to suggest changes where necessary. Choose a reward for the next appropriate behavior on your list.

By session 4, you should know which rewards are most effective. If you do not, then talk to the therapist. Also, review the previous mornings and evenings and indicate what could be improved. Talk about circumstances (e.g., inconsistency between you and your spouse) that interfered with your use of rewards.

Homework

Homework assignments after sessions 3–4 may include the following:

- Adjust as necessary the list of commands you give to each child.
- Implement changes to the morning and evening routines and follow the routines closely.
- Implement the punishments for the next-highest-severity behavior when it occurs.
- Implement the rewards for the absence of the next-highest-severity behavior.
- Engage in forced school attendance and daytime procedures if necessary and according to the therapist's recommendations.
- Continue to complete the daily logbooks, noting any specific issues or situations that arise during the week.

Sessions 5–6: Advanced Maturing of Treatment

This section describes advanced maturing of treatment. This means taking a hard look into what is currently happening in your home and what remains to be done. By this time, all the daily procedures (i.e., routines, consequences, forced attendance) should be "up and running" and finely tuned to your family's situation. At this point, you and the therapist should have an open discussion of what remains to be done and change what may be blocking treatment success. These later sessions sometimes call for more creativity, and you and the therapist may need to come up with innovative modifications of the techniques described here. For example, you may need to be creative about bringing your child to school, leaving your child's classroom, dealing with tantrums in public places, or giving rewards for attendance after school.

The basic techniques discussed earlier—commands, routines, and consequences—will continue to be addressed in these sessions. Other procedures such as forced school attendance and daytime consequences may be broadened as well. Remember that, for children who are progressing slowly, repetition of previous procedures might be appropriate.

Changing Parent Commands

The therapist will continue to review the commands you are giving to your child. Be sure to talk about things that interfere with clear commands. If you have a spouse, discuss things that interfere with a united front that you can present to your child. If necessary, examine what may be interfering with your commands (e.g., distractions) and/or ask your child to repeat what you have said to him or her. Use your child's feedback to make changes if necessary. In this example, **M** refers to the mother, and **C** refers to the child.

M: Matthew, turn off the television and get ready for school. I want you to put your jacket on and pick up your books now.

C: What? In a minute.

M: Look at me. (Mother establishes eye contact with the child.) Thank you. What did I say?

C: Come here?

M: Listen to me. Shut off the television now. (Child does so.) Thank you. Look at me. Put on your jacket and pick up your books now. What did I say?

C: Put on my jacket and get my books.

M: Thank you for listening. Go ahead.

You should also note special circumstances that break down the effectiveness of parent commands. For example, many children who refuse school for attention are members of single-parent families. Therefore, another parent is not there to back up the single parent or help deal with other children as the single parent focuses on the child who refuses school. If this is the case, using others such as siblings, the ex-spouse, or even school officials to give commands or bring the child to school may be helpful. This may be difficult, and you should not do anything that makes you uncomfortable (e.g., contact an estranged ex-spouse). However, parent commands are often more effective if they are backed up with valid promises of consequences (e.g., punishments, forced school attendance) from two parents/adults.

In addition, parent commands sometimes break down when several children in a household refuse school at once. For example, a 7-year-old may start refusing school after seeing his 9-year-old brother refuse school and get a lot of parent attention as a result. It may be useful to address the oldest child first. The older child may be the one with the most severe behavior and may be the leader of the household rebellion. In such a case, parents may need to concentrate their best efforts on issuing appropriate commands to the older child. A reduction of the older child's school refusal behavior may serve as a model for younger children. However, parents should be careful not to completely ignore younger siblings who refuse to go to school. If you have this situation in your household, be sure to discuss with the therapist all the relevant family dynamics that may influence treatment (e.g., a younger child idolizing and imitating an older one).

Finally, parent commands will be ineffective, of course, if a parent chooses not to give them. If this is the case, the therapist may look at family communications and parent moods and attitudes that break down treatment. In some cases, for example, family/parent problems need to be solved first. Such problems might include marital dissatisfaction, family conflict, alcohol/drug use, financial pressures, or other stressors. In other cases, a parent may deliberately sabotage the treatment process or otherwise fail to follow through with treatment. If any of these problems apply to you or your family, be honest with the therapist and address them right away.

At this point in treatment, you should be constantly reviewing what you are saying to your child. In particular, you should review your commands at different points of the day to see if they are clear, consistent, and effective. Compare the commands you give in the morning with those you give in the late afternoon and evening. In particular, you should be able and willing to identify bad commands and discuss how to change them. Search for anything that breaks down the effectiveness of your commands. Ideally, this review process should occur in evening conversations about the day (and/or before the next morning). If you have a spouse, you should also concentrate on supporting one another during this difficult process. The therapist may discuss how you and your spouse communicate, if you wish.

By this time in treatment, you should be clear and brief in the commands you give to your child. Commands should be few in number and be given in a neutral manner. Rewards and punishments, already set up by this point, should immediately follow obedience and disobedience to these commands, respectively. For example, if your child appropriately complies with a command, you and your spouse should praise the child quickly but not too extensively. Your child should come to realize that attention will be paid to compliance, but it is important not to dilute the value of the attention by giving too much of it. If your child does not comply with a command, then give appropriate negative consequences (e.g., time-out, working through misbehavior, ignoring).

At this point in treatment, it may also be helpful to explore with the therapist how your child's teacher interacts with your child at school. If the teacher or other school officials seem to interact with your child effectively, then no intervention is necessary. However, if your child is defiant in the school setting, then it may be helpful to include your child's teacher in the therapy process. Of course, this decision ultimately rests with you, and all ramifications should be considered. For example, including the teacher may embarrass a family member and interfere with treatment. An alternative strategy is to have the therapist meet with the teacher separately (with your permission). In this way, basic elements of treatment can be transferred to the school setting to reduce your child's behavior problems there. For example, the teacher may be instructed to give your child short, clear commands and send a daily report home to you. You may then give positive and negative consequences based on this report.

Setting Up Regular Routines

As in prior sessions, the therapist will continue to work with you to structure the daily routines for your child. By this time, the routines should be predictable to your child, and you should be providing immediate consequences for any substantial deviations from the routine. You may wish to ask your child what he or she thinks of the daily routines, but keep this conversation to a minimum. Use your child's feedback to make changes if necessary, but don't allow your child to dominate this process or negotiate changes. Remember that you are in charge of the routines at home.

Morning Routine

At this point in treatment, your child should be rising at a specific time in the morning and getting ready for school. This should be done even if he or she is not currently going to school. Specific times for each task in the morning should also be set. If your child is sticking to the morning routine, then you should praise him or her in the morning and evening. If your child is not sticking to the morning routine, then you should be giving punishments. This may be an immediate punishment (e.g., verbal reprimand in the morning) and/or a delayed punishment (e.g., grounding in room after school and at night).

During the morning routine, you should be paying attention to positive behaviors and ignoring or working through negative behaviors. If your child throws a temper tantrum, for example, you should try to dress the child and complete other morning tasks as much as possible. If this takes most of the morning, including school time, that is fine. You should try to bring your child to school in mid-morning or even mid-afternoon if necessary. The key is to give your child the clear message that school attendance is mandatory and will be pursued even after school has started that day. This will require a lot of effort on your part and may need to be coordinated with school personnel.

At this point in treatment, you should expect your child to go to school after the morning routine. School attendance may be part-time or in an alternative classroom setting (e.g., library), but your child should be spending at least part of the day at school. If your child was acting out in the morning before going to school at the start of treatment, then attendance should continue. By this point in treatment, you may use forced school attendance if appropriate.

If your child complains of physical symptoms early in the day, it may be hard to tell whether the symptoms are real. If you haven't done so, have your child checked by a medical doctor. If you have been ignoring your child's exaggerated complaints, you may have noticed that one of two things is happening. First, your child may have stopped or at least decreased his or her excessive complaints of physical symptoms. In this case, maintain what you have been doing. Second, your child may have increased his or her behavior or started complaining of more serious symptoms to elicit your sympathy. In this case, you may have to set more definitive rules. Be sure to consult the therapist and medical doctor before implementing any procedure.

It is useful to require school attendance unless your child has a fever of at least 100 degrees, and/or obviously has a physical condition that precludes school attendance (e.g., vomiting, bleeding, severe diarrhea or cough, lice). Of course, your situation may be unique and call for a different approach. Inform your child of these rules and adhere to them closely. Don't be surprised if he or she tests the limits of these rules. If your child is legitimately sick and must stay home from school, be sure that he or she is restricted to bed (not just the bedroom, but bed) for the entire school day. You should give very little extra verbal or physical attention and you should tell your child that you expect him or her to attend school the next day (if appropriate). If your child has to miss school for some other reason (e.g., family funeral), he or she should be told the same thing and attend school as soon as possible.

Daytime Routine

If school attendance is not possible at this point, then daytime routines and consequences should be used. You should make arrangements for your child during the day if the school refusal situation is unchanged and neither one of you can be at home. In this case, bring your child to work and assign him or her boring tasks or make him or her sit in a chair all day (with little verbal or physical attention from others), or to a friend, relative, or neighbor who can do the same thing.

In other cases, at least one parent or adult will need to supervise the child while at home during the day. During this time, you should give your child no extra verbal or physical attention. In addition, you should require him or her to sit alone, do boring chores, or complete homework sent home from school. The goal is to deprive children of attention for refusing school but, at the same time, make them expend some effort for their disruptive behavior and/or maintain their schoolwork. If possible, you should try to get your child to attend school each day if only for an hour or two. Repeat the *Go to school* command each hour, and follow with appropriate rewards for school attendance and punishments for school refusal.

Evening Routine

If your child stayed home for the entire day, do not allow him or her to enjoy fun activities at night. Some parents allow their children to go out and play after the normal school period is ended, but this may give the child the impression that all he or she has to do is "wait it out" to enjoy fun activities. Instead, get your child's schoolwork from the teacher and have your child work on it at night. Suspend activities such as television, video games, or other social engagements as appropriate. Consult the therapist about what to do in your case.

Whether or not your child attends school that day, his or her routine should also be set after school hours and at night. After-school activities, homework, and recreational activities should be set to a specific time and tied to school attendance. For example, if your child eventually attended school but refused to move in the morning for ten minutes to avoid school, he or she may be grounded for the evening, required to do additional homework, and/or be sent to bed early. You can ground your child or make him or sit on the stairs or in a corner at night for twice the amount of time he or she refused school that morning (e.g., 20-minute morning tantrum = 40 minutes of grounding that evening). Conversely, if your child attended school with no problems, then you may give a lot of verbal attention and spend extra time with him or her. You should make it clear to your child that school attendance is an important part of life. Any missed time will have consequences not just for that morning, but during the day, night, and even the weekend. For example, some children end up owing their parents a large "debt" of grounding time during the week. This debt can then be paid in grounding or extra chores on the weekend.

When implementing routines and administering punishments for a child with persistent school refusal behavior, some family members feel guilt and frustration and find that their home resembles a battlefield. Other family members may feel that the treatment procedures are too mechanical for their family. Although you should maintain pressure on your school refusal child during the week, you also need to maintain family cohesion and childhood fun. In some persistent cases, it may be necessary for families to set aside treatment procedures on the weekend and enjoy some fun activities together. Because the therapist knows your situation well by this point, consult with him or her.

Forced School Attendance

If you are physically bringing your child to school, continue to follow the procedures from sessions 3–4. If the situation is not improving or is becoming unbearable for you, then speak to the therapist about changing or ending the procedure. Remember, however, that ending the procedure at this point may convey to your child that his or her extreme misbehavior is enough to force you to give in. This will damage any future attempts to bring your child to school.

In some cases, parents find it emotionally difficult to force a child to attend school for an entire day. In other cases, it is simply impossible to get the child to attend full-time. In still other cases, the child has some anxiety about attending school all day but the anxiety is not severe enough to justify a full day's absence. If any of these cases describes your situation, it may be useful to bring your child to school during the afternoon and let him or her finish the school day. On subsequent days, bring your child to school at earlier and earlier times (e.g., one-half hour earlier each day until the normal beginning time is reached). An advantage of this approach is that your child may have an easier time going to school at lunchtime or recess when he or she can be with friends and when separating from you is not as difficult. In addition, your child knows that he or she has to attend school for only a couple of hours before coming home.

The disadvantage of this approach is that others may wonder why your child is starting school in the middle of the day and ask your child intrusive questions. Your child may need some strategies to cope with this situation. Examples include deflecting the questions by changing the topic or laughing with peers, declining to answer on the basis of privacy (i.e., it's none of their business), straightforwardly answering the questions, or referring the questions to someone else.

Another strategy is to have your child stay in a library or other area of school before physically bringing him or her into the classroom. This requires cooperation with school officials who must be consulted beforehand. For example, your child could stay at the library and complete schoolwork or chores (e.g., reshelving books) for the entire day. Subsequently, he or she could be reintegrated into the classroom for an initially short (e.g., one hour), and then a gradually longer, period of time. Any behavior problems on your child's part should be conveyed to you for appropriate consequences in the evening.

Another problem with forced school attendance is that some school officials are unable or unwilling to help parents bring a child into school or check the child's school attendance throughout the day. In these cases, it may be good for parents to get to know teachers, counselors, attendance officers, and others who can help to some extent. If absolutely necessary, parents can bring their child into the classroom and monitor him or her themselves. Parents can then gradually reduce the amount of time they are in the classroom. *Keep in mind, however, that parent attendance at school is exactly what many attention-seeking children want, so the procedure must be used with great care.* Do not use this procedure unless the therapist recommends it and you are confident that you can leave your child's classroom at a pace set with the therapist. If at all possible, however, avoid this procedure.

Excessive Reassurance-Seeking

In many cases, excessive reassurance-seeking continues to be a problem. Excessive reassurance-seeking may come in several forms, including (a) constantly asking the same question(s) over and over, (b) attending school but constantly telephoning parents at home or work, and/or (c) attending school but constantly demanding attention from the teacher or deliberately becoming disruptive to be sent home.

Children will sometimes repeat statements or ask the same question(s) over and over about the following topics:

- pleas for home schooling or to change teachers, schools, or classes,
- proposed deals to delay school attendance or to stop the therapy process (e.g., *I'll go to school next week if you let me go to work with you this week* or *I'll go to school tomorrow if we don't have to go to the clinic anymore*).
- physical complaints and fatigue,
- scheduling of dropoffs and pickups during the day, and
- difficulty and scheduling of schoolwork.

If your child asks the same question(s) over and over, try the following plan. When your child asks the question, answer it one time. If your child asks again, calmly remind him or her only once that he or she knows the answer. If your child asks the question again, turn away. For example:

C: Mom, are you going to make me go to school on Monday?

P: Yes, we talked about that in therapy. (Ten minutes or so pass.)

C: Are you sure I have to go on Monday? Can't I just start on Tuesday?

P: You know the answer to that question.

C: How about if I do work at home on Monday and then start Tuesday?

(Parent turns away from child. When the child begins to speak about other topics, or continues on a more appropriate discussion regarding school, the parent turns back to the child and continues to give attention.)

The therapist may set a limit on the number of times your child can ask a particular question. One rule for young children with excessive reassurance-seeking behavior is to allow one question about school per hour. Following this question and your answer, ignore your child's school-related questions until the following hour. Gradually increase this period of time (e.g., to 2, 3, 4 hours). Keep in mind, however, that this sometimes requires a lot of stamina and selective deafness.

Another form of excessive reassurance-seeking is when children attend school but constantly telephone you at home or work to get comfort about what worries them. Sometimes this is the original school refusal problem, and sometimes it develops after a child resumes school attendance. Either way, it is an inappropriate way to get attention. In most of these cases, the child should be allowed one telephone call per day to a parent and only as a reward for good classroom behavior. In severe cases, this may start with more calls and then be gradually cut back. Of course, telephone calls would have to be set up with the cooperation of school officials. You should punish excess calls at night. In addition, reassurance-seeking children should not have access to cellular telephones.

Finally, a child who attends school may seek constant attention from a teacher to be sent to the nurse's office, to be sent home from school, or to contact his or her parents. In other cases, a child will engage in disruptive behavior to be suspended from school or be otherwise sent home. In these cases, the therapist will work with you and the teacher to set up rewards and punishments in the classroom for your child's behavior. For example, a card system may be set up so that each violation of the rules (including inappropriately bothering the teacher) results in a card change from green (acceptable) to yellow (warning) to orange (last warning) to red. Upon receiving a red card, the child would be sent to the principal's office for discipline or to complete homework. In cases of older children or adolescents, more age-appropriate methods should be used (e.g., token economy, verbal feedback and reprimands, detention). A key aspect of this plan, however, is to prevent the child from leaving school, which would only serve to reinforce the child's misbehavior. Therefore, close cooperation with school officials is essential. In addition, a daily report card may be sent home so that you can administer appropriate rewards or punishments at night.

Setting Up Punishments for School Refusal Behavior

The therapist will continue to review your punishments and make changes where necessary. If appropriate, get feedback from your child about the effectiveness of the punishments and use this feedback to make changes if necessary. Talk with the therapist about any daytime restrictions on your child's activities and your attention toward him or her. Extend punishments to the second-highest-severity behavior if appropriate.

Setting Up Rewards for School Attendance

The therapist will continue to review your rewards and make changes where necessary. If appropriate, get feedback from your child about the effectiveness of the rewards and use this feedback to make changes if necessary. Extend rewards to the absence of the second-highest-severity behavior if appropriate. Be sure your child knows of all rewards and punishments beforehand.

Homework

Homework assignments after sessions 5–6 may include the following:

- Adjust the list of commands you give to each child.
- Continue to implement the morning, daytime, and night routines.
- Implement punishments for the next highest-severity behavior if it occurs.
- Implement rewards for the absence of the next highest-severity behavior.
- Continue to complete the daily logbooks, noting any specific issues or situations that arise during the week.

Sessions 7–8: Completing Treatment

In treatment sessions 7–8, treatment may begin to change in some key ways. First, as your family nears the end of therapy, it is important that the treatment procedures closely resemble what should be occurring naturally. For example, your child should be entering school on his or her own without much help. In addition, any rewards you give to your child should be based more on verbal praise. Also, you may ease the strictness of morning and evening routines if necessary and appropriate. However, be careful not to stray too much from treatment procedures that helped your child return to school.

Second, you and the therapist may extend treatment to related problems if your child's school refusal behavior is fully or nearly resolved. For example, the therapist may want to concentrate on commands you give your child at other times (e.g., weekends) or for other behavior problems. You and the therapist should not extend these treatment practices, however, until your child's school refusal behavior is under control.

As you move toward session 8, treatment can be finalized and you can discuss the end of therapy. Also, the therapist will want to give you recommendations for handling your child's behavior in the near and distant future. The therapist may develop lists of problems to avoid and, if necessary, schedule long-term follow-up contact and booster sessions (see Chapter 8).

Changing Parent Commands

The therapist will continue to review the commands that you give to your child. If your child continues to have trouble going to school or understanding what you say, the therapist may help you make changes in your commands. For some children, for example, parent commands must be kept simple and compliance must be rewarded one command at a time. To see if you have a firm grasp of good commands, the therapist may give you a hypothetical example of a child behavior and ask you to respond to it. If problems arise, the therapist will review material from previous sessions to help you adjust your commands.

If your child is attending school on a near-regular basis, your morning commands should not change. If you have other concerns, then talk to the therapist now. For example, some children will start to attend school and show excellent morning behaviors because their parents focused so much attention on challenging their bad behaviors. However, problems may remain at night or on the weekends and you should address them now. In addition, some children will start to attend school but continue to show attention-getting behaviors (e.g., excessive questions) in other places (e.g., supermarket). The therapist may focus on your commands and responses in these places as well. Remember that the chances of relapse are lower if you consistently use the treatment procedures for behaviors in different places and times. Finally, the therapist may help you extend treatment to other children in the family if you wish.

By session 8, the therapist may help you finalize your commands. He or she will give you a summary of the commands that are best for your child. The therapist will show how certain commands helped your child return to school. Use these as much as possible. Remember some basics about commands: simplicity, clarity, consistency, and immediate responses to listening or not listening. If desirable, develop with the therapist a written list of good commands and types of comments to avoid.

Keep in mind that some families return to old patterns of behavior after treatment ends. For example, some parents don't practice their new command skills once their child is back in school. Some parents will give their all during treatment but give up after treatment ends. In addition, some children increase their school refusal behavior after treatment ends to test their parents and force them to abandon firm commands. You should maintain contact with the therapist for some time after treatment ends. His or her support and feedback about good commands will help cut down on the chances of relapse.

Setting Up Regular Routines

The therapist will continue to work with you about morning and evening routines for your child. By now, these routines should be quite predictable to your child, and you should deal with any deviations immediately. If your child continues to have problems attending school, the therapist will help you change these routines as necessary. For example, some children respond better to routines that involve just a few steps.

If your child is attending school on a near-regular basis, your morning routine should stay the same. If you have other concerns, then talk to the therapist now. For example, some children will attend school but still need a lot of structure at school or home or at night and on the weekends. Let the therapist know of any differences between the morning routine and routines for other times of the day. For any additional routines, consider your child's preferences but don't let him or her dominate discussions. You have the final say about routines.

By session 8, the therapist may help you finalize routines for morning and evening (if your child is back in school, midday routines should be unnecessary). The therapist will give you a summary of what routines are best for your child. Remember some basics about routines: regularity, predictability, and immediate responses to breaking the routine. If desirable, develop with the therapist a written summary of current routines and pitfalls to avoid (e.g., too much child influence, inflexibility, failure to give punishments and rewards).

Keep in mind that some families return to old patterns of behavior after treatment ends. For example, some parents become lax about enforcing routines once their child is back in school. This sometimes happens when parents want to give their child a break or the benefit of the doubt when minor troubles start again. Unfortunately, this often leads to a child getting more attention for inappropriate behavior (the original problem that required treatment). Remember that a basic goal of treatment has been to actively attend to positive behavior and ignore negative behavior at all times. You should continue to adhere closely to the routines, respond neutrally to your child during these routines, and work through problem behaviors. Also, be sure to downplay excessive physical complaints and work to bring your child to school at least part-time on days when he or she refuses to attend. You should maintain contact with the therapist for some time after treatment ends to prevent recurring problems.

Setting Up Punishments for School Refusal Behavior

The therapist will continue to review the punishments you give for school refusal behavior. By now, these punishments should be quite predictable to your child and be given consistently. If your child continues to have problems attending school, the therapist will help you make changes. For example, some children will respond only to punishments that are stronger, applied more immediately, or applied more consistently. If you are using daytime punishments, the therapist will also want to know their effect and help you make any necessary changes. The therapist may give you a hypothetical example of a child behavior and ask how you might respond to it using punishments and rewards. If problems arise, the therapist will review material from previous sessions to help you adjust punishments and rewards.

If your child is going to school on a near-regular basis, then the punishments should stay the same. If you have other concerns, then talk to the therapist now. For example, some children will attend school but still require punishments for related behaviors such as aggression, noncompliance in other settings, failure to complete homework, bedwetting and/or sleeping with parents, tantrums, general disruptive behavior at home or in class, arguing, and yelling, among others. If behaviors such as these remain a problem, then you should deal with them now. The chances of relapse will be less if you understand how to use punishments consistently for different behaviors.

By session 8, the therapist may help you finalize the punishments you give for school refusal behaviors and make changes where necessary (by this time, daytime punishments should no longer be needed). He or she will give you a summary of what punishments are best for your child. The therapist will show how specific punishments helped your child's return to school. Remember some basics about punishments: fairness, predictability, consistency, and immediate administration when needed. If desirable, develop with the therapist a written summary of the useful punishments and pitfalls to avoid (e.g., giving punishments too long after a specific behavior).

Keep in mind the danger of not giving punishments in the future. For example, some parents stop giving punishments because of guilt, shame, detachment, or nonchalance. Any current problems in this area should be addressed now. In addition, some parents differ in their responses to a child or to children across different behaviors. Remember that consistency is essential in giving rewards and punishments to children. Finally, some parents fall into the habit of giving severe punishment every once in a while instead of moderate, consistent, and predetermined punishments whenever they are appropriate. Some parents wait until a behavior problem is very severe before giving punishment. Be sure to use appropriate punishment every time your child misbehaves. If necessary, discuss with the therapist the use of physical punishment and its pitfalls. Keep in mind that physical punishment may increase aggression in children. Stick to the treatment procedures that the therapist outlined for you.

Setting Up Rewards for School Attendance

The therapist will continue to review the rewards you give for school attendance. By now, the rewards should be quite predictable to your child and be given consistently. If your child continues to have problems going to school, the therapist will help you change these rewards. Some children respond to rewards that are stronger, applied more immediately, or applied more consistently. If your child is attending school on a near-regular basis, then the rewards should stay the same. If you have other concerns, then talk to the therapist now. For example, rewards may be set up for the absence of the behaviors mentioned above.

By session 8, the therapist may help you finalize the rewards given for school attendance and make changes where necessary. Be careful not to become complacent about giving rewards in the future. Some parents stop giving rewards once their child is back in school, but this often leads to future relapse. In addition, some parents start to take school attendance for granted, become busy and "forget" to recognize their child's behavior, or give big but infrequent rewards. All of these practices may lead to relapse, however, and should be avoided.

Keep in mind that your child should know of any changes you decide to make in future treatment. Children should not be punished for behaviors they don't know are wrong. Remember, if you need to punish, you don't need to explain, and if you need to explain, you don't need to punish. In other words, all rules, punishments, rewards, and unwanted behaviors should be explained to your child beforehand and he or she should know them by heart.

Homework

Homework assignments after sessions 7–8 may include the following:

- Continue to use appropriate commands. Periodically review the list of pitfalls regarding commands given by the therapist.
- Continue to use the morning and evening routines. Periodically review the list of problems regarding routines given by the therapist.
- Continue to use the punishments and rewards for the most severe school refusal behaviors and related behaviors, if applicable. Periodically review the list of pitfalls given by your therapist.
- Contact the therapist as needed for support, feedback, answers to questions, long-term follow-up, and booster sessions if necessary.

Children Refusing School to Pursue Tangible Rewards Outside of School

Session 1: Starting Treatment

If your child is refusing school to pursue tangible rewards outside of school, then he or she may be hiding school absences, displaying verbal and physical aggression, running away, spending an excessive amount of time with friends, and acting disruptively to stay out of school. Your child's behaviors may also include a hostile attitude, refusal to talk, drug use, gambling, or excessive sleep. Up to now, the action your family has taken to reduce these problems may have been marked by conflict, bribery, severe punishment, and confusion about what to do next. In addition, you've probably noticed that family conflict often leads to your child's continued school refusal behavior.

You may have developed a certain way of responding to your child's disruptive behavior and other problems that affect school attendance. This treatment will teach your family a different way of coping with these problems. It will teach you skills that are alternatives to arguing and confusion. Your family will practice problem-solving techniques. At first, the things you learn may cause even more problems than before. For your family to make progress, however, it is important that everyone work hard and through difficult situations. The more everyone cooperates in therapy, the faster your family will progress in treatment.

The focus of treatment is your entire family, but especially you, your spouse if you have one, and your child who refuses school. The major goal is to change the way your family solves problems, deals with conflict, increases rewards for school attendance, and decreases rewards for school absence. Specifically, this will involve:

- setting up times and places for negotiating solutions to problems,
- defining behavior problems,
- designing written contracts between you and your child to tackle the problem, and
- implementing contracts.

The therapist will probably split the treatment time equally between you/your spouse and your child. The therapist should speak with your child first. The therapist should also mediate the first few contracts by negotiating separately with you and with your child. Speaking with the child first is sometimes key to getting him or her "on board" the treatment program. It is important for the child to know that the therapist is considering his or her view as much as the parent's view.

A key element in contracting is that everyone negotiate in good faith. This means that you and your child should give a reasonable account of what you are willing to do and what you feel is unfair or unworkable. If there is anything you feel uneasy about, say so. The therapist will ask about each line of each contract to make sure it is satisfactory to you and your child. If it isn't, you and your child should speak up and ask for changes. Siblings should be told about the treatment procedures so they know what to expect. In many cases, it is preferable to include other children in the contract process so they don't feel left out and so they can help monitor compliance.

Setting Up Times and Places to Negotiate Solutions to Problems

At this time, the therapist will probably conduct the problem-solving/contracting process entirely during the therapy session. In this way, the therapist can see how you and your child design the contract, can provide detailed suggestions, and can address any problems. In particular, the therapist will note any communication problems your family may have, as well as other behaviors (e.g., sabotage, refusal to participate) that interfere with good problem-solving. If these interfering behaviors are minor, the therapist may address them now. For example, if one family member has trouble expressing what he or she wants, the therapist can give some suggestions for responding. However, if these interfering behaviors are major (e.g., fighting), the therapist may want to assess them further and address them over several sessions.

Although much of the problem-solving/contracting process will initially take place in session, you and your child should think about times and places that your family can talk about problems at home during the week. In later treatment sessions, contracting should take place during these times at home. Think about times when everyone is home, when other matters are not too urgent, when family members are relaxed, and when there are no immediate distractions. This is often a difficult, if not impossible, task. However, making time for problem-solving is essential if your family's conflict and your child's school refusal behavior are to be reduced. If you have problems finding such a time, be sure to inform the therapist so that he or she can address this in session. A common problem is when a family member doesn't want to participate in family meetings because he or she fears that other family members will "gang up" on him or her.

Defining the Behavior Problem

When designing the first contract for your family, the therapist will want to focus on a problem other than your child's school refusal behavior. Although this may seem counterintuitive, it is essential that family members practice appropriate problem-solving on a simpler level at least once. This will help the therapist gauge how fast or slow further treatment needs to be. Setting aside school refusal behavior for the moment may also lessen immediate family tension and pressure on your child.

The therapist may choose a minor problem that has recently occurred. Examples include not doing chores, not going to bed on time, not checking in with a parent, or not completing a homework assignment. The therapist will ask your family to tackle only one problem. Try to avoid problems that are unsolvable, long-standing, or overly complicated. For example, don't focus on your child's trouble with the law a year ago (now unsolvable), your family's conflict (which may be long-standing), or your family's finances (too complicated). Keep it simple.

When defining a problem, each family member should participate. Different family members may define a problem differently, but this is normal. For example, you might define a problem as "He never takes out the garbage when I ask him." Your child might define the problem as "I have to take out the garbage all the time." Each definition is vague, however, and points to a communication problem. As a compromise, your therapist might describe the problem simply as "The garbage is not being taken out on a regular basis." In this case, no one is blamed and the problem is clearly defined.

Designing a Contract

As previously mentioned, the therapist should mediate the first contract by negotiating separately with you and with your child. In this way, the therapist can engage in "shuttle diplomacy" by working his or her way back and forth between you and your child. After the behavior problem has been well-defined, the therapist will ask your child to describe as many potential solutions to the problem as possible. Even humorous ones such as "Hiring a maid to take out the garbage" should be included. The therapist will ask your child to come up with 5–10 proposed solutions and rank them in order of desirability. Desirability depends on whether the solution is practical, realistic, specific, and agreeable to everyone. After completing this process with your child, the therapist will ask you to come up with your own solutions and rank them in order of desirability.

The therapist will then propose one solution that is most desirable. All of you should bargain in good faith and let the therapist know if the solution is acceptable or not. Focus on compromise. For example, a good solution to the problem presented here might be: "(Child) will be asked to take out the garbage only on Wednesday and Saturday, but must take out the garbage when asked on those days." If you and your child agree to this solution, then the therapist will move to the next step.

The next step is to develop rewards and punishments for completing or not completing the contract. As before, the therapist will speak with you and your child separately and focus on rewards and punishments that are desirable and agreeable to everyone. The first contract will be simple. For example:

________ (Child) agrees to take out the garbage on Wednesday and Saturday if asked. If ________ (child) completes this chore correctly, then ________ (child) will receive an extra half-hour of curfew on Saturday night. If ________ (child) does not complete the chore, then ________ (child) will be required to be in the house one hour earlier than usual.

As mentioned earlier, you may wish to add other children to the contract as appropriate. The therapist will then close any loopholes that might exist in the contract. In this contract, for example, it may be necessary to define exactly when the child will take out the garbage, what the chore involves, who will decide if the chore was carried out correctly, and what time curfew is supposed to be. In closing the loopholes, the therapist will give more say to the parents. In addition, the finished contract should be time-limited—no more than a few days at most. In this way, if problems arise, the therapist can address them quickly.

Implementing the Contract

Once the first contract has been designed, you and your child should read it and say whether you agree to it. If not, then the therapist will renegotiate the contract. If you reach agreement, then all of you will sign the contract and get a copy. You should display the contract in some part of the house where it can be read, referred to, and initialed daily by everyone. The door of the refrigerator is a good place. You should ask final questions at this point. Because this is the first contract, the therapist may contact your family several times in the days following this session to help you address any problems. In the meantime, reflect on what you have just accomplished. You and your child have agreed without fighting to solve a problem. If this contract is successful, you should be able to solve more difficult problems.

Homework

Homework assignments after session 1 may include the following:

- Think about times and places where you can work on problem-solving in the future.
- Think about problems and potential solutions for the next contract.
- Implement the current contract and contact the therapist if necessary.
- Continue to complete the daily logbooks, noting any specific issues or situations that arise during the week.

Session 2: Intensifying Treatment

This section describes how the therapist may intensify treatment for a child refusing school to pursue tangible rewards outside of school. As discussed before, the major focus of treatment here will be you, your spouse, and your child, although other children may be included as appropriate.

Setting Up Times and Places to Negotiate Solutions to Problems

At this time, it is still best to conduct most of the problem-solving/contracting process in the therapy session. However, your family should begin to meet at regular times at home to talk about the current contract and what changes might be made at the next therapy session. As mentioned before, these times should have little distraction and full family participation. This will allow your family to practice discussing important issues, and will help the therapy process. In later treatment, contracting will be taking place during these times at home.

For now, the therapist may ask you to schedule one or two home sessions between sessions 2–3. During the home sessions, everyone should sit at a table and talk about the contract or other issues. At first, this may be awkward, and some children may call the process "stupid." To ease tension, limit the meeting to 10–15 minutes. Also, make sure that everyone has an equal amount of time to speak. If there are four people in the family, for example, give everyone three minutes to talk about whatever they want. Keep time if necessary. Some other basic rules for the family meeting are:

- Agree ahead of time about who will call the meeting to order. Rotate this job among family members if possible and as appropriate.
- As much as possible, limit the family discussion to the contract and any complaints or problems each family member may have. Try to stick to simple statements and avoid going off on tangents. Avoid hurtful comments as much as possible.
- Allow each person to speak without interruption. If one person wants to respond to another, he or she must wait their turn. Try to minimize questioning.
- Do not allow the meeting to be dominated by one family member, especially a parent. If someone is given three minutes to talk and only one minute is used, then think about that person's statement in silence for two minutes.
- Encourage family members to stay at the meeting for its entire duration. If a family member does not wish to talk, he or she can simply sit and listen to the others.
- Praise everyone for attending the meeting.
- If the meeting does not go well, end it and schedule another at a later time. Examples of problems include insults and verbal and physical fighting. In extreme cases where family members cannot get along, then inform the therapist and discuss these issues in session.
- If the meeting goes well and a healthy discussion is taking place, feel free to extend it. However, if one person thinks the meeting is not going well, then it is not going well. You should then reschedule this meeting. An exception may occur if one family member is deliberately sabotaging or disrupting the meeting. In this case, family members should tolerate or include the disruptive person as much as possible but ask him or her to leave if necessary. The therapist should be made aware of this disruption to address it as soon as possible. As a general rule, exclusions of this sort should be kept to an absolute minimum.
- Contact the therapist during the meeting if you have questions.

Defining the Behavior Problem

The therapist will review with your family whether the first contract was successful. If you had problems, then the therapist will explore the reasons why. Be honest about why the contract may have been unsuccessful. Talk about even sensitive topics such as fighting among family members, low motivation, or deliberate failure. The therapist will spend a lot of time talking about these issues and may want to reimplement the contract. Keep in mind that some cases take longer than others to resolve. Additional practice with simpler contracts is often necessary before moving on to more complicated ones.

If the first contract was successful, then the therapist may want to move on to a second contract. This second contract may involve more complicated problems that have nothing to do with your child's school refusal behavior, or some limited aspect of school refusal behavior. The more severe a child's school refusal behavior, the greater the chance a therapist will suggest the first approach. In this way, the family has another opportunity to practice problem-solving before tackling school refusal behavior.

If the therapist believes it is appropriate to move to the next step, then the next contract may contain some aspect of school attendance behavior (e.g., morning preparation). In addition, you should talk with the therapist about other behaviors that could be in the contract. *It is a good idea to include chores because later contracts may include paying children for chores if they attend school.* In the meantime, however, talk about the chores, behaviors, or problems you and your family would like to emphasize. Again, avoid problems that are unsolvable, long-standing, or overly complicated.

You, your child, and the therapist will define each part of a new contract and come up with compromises. For example, the contract may be extended to include (a) the "garbage" chore from before, (b) preparing for school in the morning, and (c) obeying curfew (assuming that the latter two are not currently being done). *Be sure to define each part specifically.* For example, "preparing for school in the morning" might mean dressing and eating by a certain time and "obeying curfew" might mean coming home at a certain time at night. Specific times should always be set.

Designing the Contract

As before, the therapist will negotiate the new contract separately with you and with your child. Each of you should describe as many solutions to the problems as possible. Again, focus on solutions that are practical, realistic, specific, and potentially agreeable to everyone. Choose the one proposed solution that is most desirable for each problem. For getting ready in the morning, for example, a good solution might be to arrange the times at which your child will do different things (e.g., eating, dressing). With respect to curfew, a good solution might be to choose a time that is reasonable to you and your child.

If each family member agrees to the definitions, then the therapist will help you come up with rewards and punishments for completing or not completing the contract. As before, focus on those rewards and punishments that are most appropriate and agreed-upon by everyone. In addition, the therapist will close any loopholes in the contract and make sure that the contract is time-limited. You should also add a general statement to the contract to declare your family's commitment to the therapy process. A sample contract based on the issues discussed here is presented in Figure 7.1 and a blank contract is presented in Figure A.7.

Implementing the Contract

Remember that this new contract is appropriate *only* if your family successfully completed the first contract, your family is getting along fairly well, and you are reasonably sure that your family can handle all the parts of this contract. If your family's situation is different in some way (e.g., the first contract was unsuccessful), then the therapist may proceed more slowly and develop a simpler contract or ask you to reimplement the first one. For moderate to severe cases of school refusal behavior, this new contract may be appropriate because actual school attendance is not yet required. In many cases, a gradual buildup to school attendance is more effective than immediately requiring the child to attend school. For milder cases of school refusal behavior, where the child is missing school only part of the time (e.g., certain classes), this new contract or a more complicated one may be appropriate.

Once the contract has been designed, each family member should read it and state whether he or she agrees to it. If not, then the contract will be renegotiated. If everyone does agree to the contract, then everyone should sign it and receive a copy. Everyone should ask final questions at this point. Be sure to contact the therapist between sessions should any problems arise or if a family member wants to talk about important issues concerning the contract or your family. A common problem that arises is when a child agrees to the contract because he or she feels pressured to do so or because he or she is frustrated and wants to get out of the therapy session as soon as possible. It is a good idea for the therapist to contact the child that night or the next day to see if the child wants to make any changes in the contract or make known any concerns he or she has about the therapy process.

Sample Contract

Privileges	Responsibilities
General	
In exchange for decreased family conflict and a resolution to school refusal behavior, all family members agree to	try as hard as possible to maintain this contract and fully participate in therapy.
Specific	
In exchange for an extra half-hour of curfew on weekend nights, (child) agrees to	take out the garbage on Wednesday and Saturday if asked.
Should (child) not complete this responsibility,	he or she will be required to be in the house one hour earlier than usual.
In exchange for the privilege of possessing a radio and television in his or her room, (child) agrees to	rise in the morning at 7:00, dress and eat by 7:40, wash and brush teeth by 8:00, and finalize preparations for school by 8:20.
Should (child) not complete this responsibility,	he or she will lose the radio and television and be grounded for one day.
In exchange for the privilege of possessing a compact disc player in his or her room, (child) agrees to	obey 9:00 p.m. curfew on school nights and 11:00 curfew on weekend nights.
Should (child) not complete this responsibility,	he or she will lose the compact disc player and be grounded for one day.

(Child) and his or her parents agree to uphold the conditions of this contract and read and initial the contract each day.

Signature of (child) and parents:

____

______________________________ Date: ______________

Figure 7.1.

Homework

Homework assignments after session 2 may include the following:

- Set up a time and place when a family discussion can occur. Meet 1–2 times between sessions for these informal conversations. Follow the rules and record the conversation for the therapist if all family members agree.
- Think about problems and potential solutions for the next contract.
- Implement the current contract and contact the therapist as necessary.
- Write down any problems that seem to interfere with the contract.
- Continue to complete the daily logbooks, noting any specific issues or situations that arise during the week.

Sessions 3–4: Maturing of Treatment

In maturing of treatment, you and your child may revisit procedures from sessions 1–2. In addition, you will learn about communication skills training, peer refusal skills training, alternative contract ideas, and what can be done if your child continues to miss several classes during the school day. At this point in treatment, contracting should focus more specifically on your child's particular school refusal behaviors. You may also work on dealing with your child during the day if he or she skips school or remains home following tantrums or other problems. In doing so, you should begin to see an effect on your child's school refusal behavior and learn important skills that may be useful for tackling other problems in the future. Many parents learn skills that are useful in dealing with their other children as well.

Setting Up Times and Places to Negotiate Solutions to Problems

Your family should continue to meet at a regular time at home to discuss the current contract and what changes might be made at the next therapy session. At this point, you should meet about twice a week. The therapist will ask you about these informal sessions. He or she will be interested in whether the meetings have been actually scheduled and held, discussions during the meeting, conflicts, points of agreement and disagreement, compliments and insults, silence among certain family members, and areas that need improvement. If you have numerous problems, the therapist may listen to an audiotape of the meetings, ask you to change or stop the meetings, and/or conduct more in-depth family therapy in session. If the meetings are progressing fairly well, your family should continue them during the week. By session 4, your family should practice negotiating with one another just like you do in the therapy session. This will enhance problem-solving and communication skills training.

Communication Skills Training

In communication skills training, family members are taught to have conversations without verbal abuse, hostility, negative thinking, interruptions, or dismissals of each other's statements. At this point in treatment, the therapist may teach these skills if your family fights frequently and/or if miscommunication is interfering with the contracting process.

Communication skills training initially involves having one family member make a statement to, or ask a question of, another family member who listens quietly. Following the first person's statement, the second person is asked to repeat or paraphrase what was said to make sure the message was correctly heard and understood. In the following example. **C** represents the child and **F** represents the father.

C: I feel like I can't do anything with my friends.

F: It sounds like you feel you want more time with your friends.

During this first step, the therapist will concentrate on basic problems in communication. Examples of such problems include interruptions, incorrect paraphrasing, refusal to do the task, silence, and hostile words (e.g., insults). The therapist will stop a conversation as soon as a problem develops, give feedback, and ask you to try again.

At this stage, your family should simply concentrate on giving short, clear messages; listening; and paraphrasing correctly. Your family can practice these steps in the therapy session and later during family conversations and meetings. If possible, keep a list of problems that come up during family discussions.

Defining the Behavior Problem

The therapist will review with your family the success or failure of the previous contract. If the contract failed, he or she will explore why. Be sure to mention any family fights, motivation problems, or other factors that prevented the success of the contract. The therapist will want to spend time dealing with these issues and reimplement the contract if possible.

If the previous contract was successful, your family should be proud. Remember that problems can be peacefully and effectively solved. Depending on your situation, the next contract could involve either more complex problems that have nothing to do with school refusal behavior, or the introduction of school refusal behavior as one key part. The more severe your child's school refusal behavior or your family's fighting, the more likely the therapist will use the first approach.

If your family is progressing well, then the next contract may focus more on your child's school attendance. One of the best ways to do this is to link house chores, money, and school attendance. This must be done with caution and is subject to your approval, your family's financial situation, and whether the extra work and rewards are acceptable to you and your child. The therapist will help your family develop a list of appropriate chores and behaviors and then use this list to set conditions of the new contract. If you object to using chores or money, then you will need to explore other rewards and punishments with the therapist.

During session 4, the therapist will review the success or failure of this contract. Because this contract was the first to deal specifically with school attendance, the therapist will explore at length any problems that prevented the contract from succeeding. Many children fulfill their end of a contract *until* school attendance is required. At this point, many children begin to say one thing and do another. For example, it is not unusual for a child to agree to school attendance in the therapy session but miss school the next day. In this case, the therapist will look for the cause of such failure.

Peer Refusal Skills Training

A common reason for such failure is peer pressure to skip school. Your child may fully intend to go to school but, once he or she is there, others tempt or goad him or her into skipping school. The therapist may find it useful to teach your child to use peer refusal skills to resist such pressure. Peer refusal skills training meshes nicely with communication skills training because the therapist focuses on talking to others in a more constructive way. To start, the therapist may ask your child to describe what his or her peers say to try to get him or her to skip school. In the following example, **T** represents the therapist and **C** represents the child.

T: Okay, Justin, you're saying that you meant to go to school, but that your friends kind of pressured you to skip yesterday afternoon?

C: Yeah, they found me in the hallway and kept after me to join them off-campus for lunch. Then we just hung out and blew off the afternoon.

T: What did your friends say to you to get you to skip school?

C: I don't know, they just ragged on me. They kept saying we'd have fun and that we'd do our work later. They said we'd just have lunch for a couple of hours, but then it turned into the whole day.

The therapist and your child may then create statements that your child can use to firmly but appropriately refuse offers to skip school. The therapist will take into account your child's fear of social rejection and build responses that will not let your child lose face. It is helpful sometimes for youth to blame their school attendance on their parents or therapist, thus absolving them (temporarily only) of blame. In addition, a child can talk to peers about his or her interest in a particular class, the need to finish uncompleted work, potential rewards for school attendance, or a lack of desire to skip school. At this point in therapy, the therapist may find it useful to outline suggested responses to peer pressures and ask your child to try them at school if the need arises. For example:

T: Okay, Justin, we've talked about some ways you can avoid being in situations where your friends can pressure you into leaving school. We'll also work, as you agreed, on changing your lunch schedule so you'll eat earlier and see them less. But let's assume that your friends do track you down during the day and get after you to skip school. What can you say to them?

C: I don't know, maybe I don't want to or maybe I can't?

T: Okay, you could say that, but you're not giving a definite reason. I'm afraid that if you say "I don't want to," they'll think you're thinking about it and keep after you. What are some specific reasons you can give, like focusing on your parents or talking about your schoolwork?

C: I guess I could say my parents are really on my case about school and I should go. Or I could say I have to finish my science project that's due. I guess I could even just say "Some other time" and walk away.

T: Great! Let's try those in case you do run into friends who ask you to skip school. Let's see how it works over the next few days, and I'll call you to see how it goes.

Remember that peer refusal skills training will likely be most helpful if peer pressure is the main cause of interference with the school attendance contract. In addition, these skills may be helpful for refusing offers of drugs, which may be linked to school absence. However, if the contract is failing simply because your child is giving "lip service" in session to you or the therapist, then peer refusal skills may not be helpful and a more intensive treatment alternative may be necessary.

Designing the Contract

As before, the therapist will focus on negotiation, compromise, and assurances that the contract is acceptable to everyone. In addition, he or she will emphasize clear solutions, effective rewards and punishments, closed loopholes, and a short timeline. This new contract should closely mirror the previous contract but with necessary changes. In addition, the therapist may tie communication skills training to the contracting procedure. For example, he or she may bring your family together to form the contract and practice listening and paraphrasing. A sample contract based on issues discussed earlier (see Defining the Behavior Problem) is presented in Figure 7.2.

Keep in mind that full-time school attendance does not necessarily have to be pursued at this point. Sometimes asking the child to simply attend a few of their favorite classes per day is a good start.

If your family does not approve of linking money to chores and school attendance, then alternative contract ideas may be proposed. Examples of alternative tangible rewards include extension of curfew, more time with friends, fewer required chores, eating by oneself or with friends, shopping, video games and movies, car rides to school, and certain foods, among others.

Implementing the Contract

This sample contract is appropriate only if your family has done well to this point. If your family struggled with this contract, then the therapist will repeat procedures from sessions 1–2. The timeline for this contract should be short and the next therapy session should be scheduled within 3–5 days. This will give your family time to implement the contract and allow the therapist to suggest changes if problems arise. *In many cases, the first contract dealing specifically with school refusal behavior is the most difficult to implement.* Therefore, be sure to rely on the therapist for support and feedback. Parts of previous contracts (e.g., curfew) may also be added to this contract if you like.

Escorting Your Child to School

Despite the contract, your child may still not fulfill his or her part. Many children will agree to school attendance but skip school during the day anyway without peer pressure. As a result, appropriate rewards are never given and the child continues to pursue inappropriate rewards outside of school.

If this is your situation, it may be necessary to walk your child from class to class during the day. School officials are often unable to monitor children during the day, so you (or your spouse or another adult you trust) may need to do so. This requires a lot of effort and time on someone's part. However, the procedure is often effective because it ensures school attendance and allows a child to earn appropriate rewards. In addition, the potential embarrassment is sometimes

Sample Contract

Privileges	Responsibilities
General	
In exchange for decreased family conflict and a resolution to school refusal behavior, all family members agree to	try as hard as possible to maintain this contract and fully participate in therapy.
Specific	
In exchange for the privilege of being paid to complete household chores between now and the next therapy session, (child) agrees to:	attend school full-time between now and the next therapy session.
Should (child) not complete this responsibility,	he or she will be required to complete the household chores without being paid.
In exchange for the privilege of possessing a radio and television in his or her room, (child) agrees to	rise in the morning at 7:00, dress and eat by 7:40, wash and brush teeth by 8:00, and finalize preparations for school by 8:20.
Should (child) not complete this responsibility,	he or she will lose the radio and television and be grounded for one day.
In exchange for compensation of five dollars, (child) agrees to:	vacuum the living room and clean the bathroom between now and the next therapy session.
Should (child) not complete this responsibility, or complete the responsibility in an insufficient manner (to be determined by parents),	he or she will not be paid.

(Child) and his or her parents agree to uphold the conditions of this contract and read and initial the contract each day.

Signature of (child) and parents:

____

______________________________ Date: ______________

Figure 7.2.

enough to prompt school attendance. At this stage in treatment, the therapist may simply suggest this procedure as an option for your family (including your child) to consider if the next few school attendance contracts do not succeed. However, if there is some urgency in getting your child back to school, you may use escorting now. Be sure to discuss this procedure with the therapist before starting.

Homework

Homework assignments after sessions 3–4 may include the following:

- Continue to meet informally as a family once or twice between now and the next session. Discuss the parts of the current contract that remain a problem and those that are most effective. Also discuss how family members communicate and what should change. Record the conversation for the therapist if desirable. Practice communication skills as appropriate.
- Think about problems and potential solutions for the next contract.
- Implement the current contract and contact the therapist if necessary.
- Begin to use peer refusal skills and escorting as appropriate.
- Continue to complete the daily logbooks, noting any specific issues or situations that arise during the week.

Sessions 5–6: Advanced Maturing of Treatment

In sessions 5–6, advanced maturing of treatment should take place. The basic elements of contracting—defining problems and negotiating solutions—will continue to be the focus of these sessions. However, other procedures such as communication skills training and peer refusal skills training may be broadened as well. Remember that, for children who are progressing more slowly, repetition of previous procedures might be appropriate. You should take a hard look into what is happening in your home and what remains to be done. By this time, all the daily procedures (i.e., family meetings, contracts, refusal skills) should be "up and running" and finely tuned to your family's situation. At this point, you and the therapist should have an open discussion of what remains to be done and change what may be blocking treatment success. In addition, these later sessions sometimes call for more creativity, and you and the therapist should try to create innovative modifications of the techniques described here. For example, you may need to be inventive about certain parts of a contract, increasing or enhancing family communication, or helping a child refuse offers to skip school.

Setting Up Times and Places to Negotiate Solutions to Problems

The therapist will review your family meetings that have been taking place at home. In particular, he or she will explore how well your family negotiated solutions to problems and will analyze audiotapes of the meetings if necessary. The therapist will check to see if family members were able to listen to one another and correctly repeat or paraphrase each other's messages. The therapist will check for interruptions, incorrect paraphrasing, insults, and silence, among other behaviors. If you made a list of communication problems, discuss it with the therapist. If your family had problems with the first step in communication skills training, then the therapist will continue to build listening and paraphrasing skills. Keep in mind that, if your family is having extreme problems communicating, then more extensive family therapy and exploration of other issues might be appropriate and can supplement the procedures described here.

Advanced Communication Skills Training

Techniques

If your family did listen and paraphrase well over the past few days or sessions, then you may go on to the next step in communication skills training. This might involve practicing conversations without hostility. To start, the therapist may suggest certain rules about what you should avoid in a conversation. He or she will encourage family members to avoid name calling, insults, sarcasm, inappropriate suggestions, and screaming, among other behaviors. If these behaviors are not a problem, then the therapist may address less serious problems (e.g., lack of eye contact, articulation).

Conversations between family members should first be short, involve two family members only, and be closely monitored by the therapist. He or she will use a role-play and feedback procedure that will be explained to each family member. This might first involve a conversation between one family member and the therapist in front of other family members. In the following example, the therapist plays the role of the father speaking to his teenage son. This technique is especially advisable if two family members are having severe problems communicating with one another or haven't done so in a long time. The intention is to have the other party (in this case, the father) and other family members model an appropriate conversation.

C: I just don't understand why I have to go to school. I'm almost 16 years old and everybody keeps treating me like a little kid.

T: (Acting as father and looking directly at the child) It sounds like you're kind of angry.

C: Yeah, I am. Why can't you just leave me alone to do my own thing?

T: Can you be more specific? I'm not sure what you mean.

C: I want to spend more time with my friends. I should be able to go out if I want to.

T: Okay, it sounds to me like you feel confined and feel that you don't spend enough time with your friends—is that right?

C: Yeah, why can't I do what I have to do at home and then go out without a hassle?

After this brief role-play, the therapist will point out to everyone the appropriate behavior that was demonstrated: calmness of tone, lack of interruptions, acknowledging another person's viewpoint, correct paraphrasing, and lack of insults or other derogatory remarks. In this example, the therapist/father gathered information from the teenager without judgment or defensiveness. The problem (i.e., time with friends) was identified and defined accurately and negative emotions were vented appropriately.

During this role-play, be sure to raise any questions you may have. The therapist may practice a one-on-one conversation with your child to reinforce some important points (e.g., listening). Later, two family members (e.g., father, son) may be asked to speak directly to one another in a short conversation. The therapist will monitor this conversation closely and interrupt and give feedback if problems develop. For example:

C: Well, like I said before, I always get hassled and don't spend enough time with my friends.

F: I don't get it, you're with your friends all the time.

T: Mr. Williams, try to repeat what your son just said.

F: He said he doesn't spend enough time with his friends.

T: Good. Let's find out exactly what concerns your son. (Motions to do so.)

F: Okay. What exactly concerns you?

C: I do my chores and homework, so then I should be allowed to see my friends. Now that I have to go to school more, I don't get to see them that often.

F: Okay, how much time do you feel you need to spend with your friends? (Therapist nods to approve of this statement.)

C: I don't know, maybe a couple of hours a night. What's the big deal about that?

T: Okay, John, let's stick to answering the question. Try to leave out statements or questions that are sarcastic or too negative.

C: Okay. I'd like to spend at least a couple of hours a night with my friends. Maybe some more time on the weekends. (Therapist nods.)

F: Okay, so two hours a night on a school night after chores and homework and dinner are done? Does that sound about right?

C: Yeah.

The therapist will introduce different issues in these dialogues between two family members to help you practice appropriate communications. The therapist will make a recommendation about how long to practice these brief conversations before taking the next step. The next step could be other one-on-one conversations (e.g., mother-child) or adding more people to the conversation. Once a particular parent-child dialogue is progressing well, for example, the other parent may be added. You should be careful, however, to avoid overly strict alliances (e.g., two parents versus one child) that could damage the communication process. Should problems occur, the therapist will again step in and give feedback. For example:

C: When I'm with my friends, I should be able to do what I want.

F: Okay, it sounds like you want more freedom. Is that right?

C: Yeah, I guess so. I'm almost an adult.

F: Well, you're getting there . . .

M: (To father:) Frank, he's not an adult.

F: I realize that, but John seems to feel he's becoming an adult. (To child:) Right?

C: Yeah, and so I should be able to do what I want.

M: Well, you can't do anything you want. Your father and I will discuss what you can and can't do.

T: Okay, Mrs. Williams, let's focus on paraphrasing what John just said and then gathering information about it.

M: Okay, he said he wants to do what he wants. (To child:) What kinds of things do you want to do? (Therapist nods.)

If your family has done well listening, paraphrasing, and having short conversations without many problems, then communication skills training may advance even further. This might involve practicing extended conversations that are increasingly constructive in nature. As before, this will include role-play and feedback in which the therapist first demonstrates an extended, constructive conversation with another family member. As the family practices these extended conversations, the therapist will closely watch for negative communication.
In addition, your family may focus more on increasing compliments and other pleasantries. The therapist may also spend time helping family members reframe comments in a positive way. For example, a statement such as "You barely finished your homework" may be translated into "I really like it when you finish your schoolwork on time."

Potential Problems

Several things may prevent communication skills training from working quickly or at all. These include pessimism, punishment of one converser, and silence. In many cases of severe school refusal behavior, family members have been fighting for several months or years. As a result, they have set negative patterns of talking and are pessimistic about change. It is important for family members to see that they can learn to interact well at a simple level and that this signals hope for future change. Therefore, extended practice at this stage may be necessary, and simple positive conversations may be a realistic final goal. A second problem occurs when one family member continually criticizes another during a conversation. In this situation, the therapist may act as a mediator by allowing one person to speak, paraphrasing the message himself or herself, and then presenting it to the second person. Be sure to raise any unresolved family issues that cause hostile conversations between family members. Finally, if silence is an issue, the therapist may focus on those family members who are willing to talk and allow the silent member to watch these conversations. In a one-on-one meeting with the silent member, the therapist may try to convince that person to participate in therapy as much as possible.

Be aware that your family may not be able to change all hostile conversations in a short period of time. By this time in treatment, however, you and your family should know what makes a good conversation and what prevents a good conversation. Your family should become skilled at listening to one another and accurately paraphrasing what is said. In addition, your family should be using these new ways of communicating in your home meetings and when designing new contracts. If your family has not yet reached this point, the therapist will repeat the procedures practiced in previous sessions. Also, the therapist will continue to explore other issues and family dynamics that prevent family members from having positive conversations.

Defining the Behavior Problem

The therapist will review with your family the success or failure of the previous contract. He or she will explore at length any problems that prevented the contract from succeeding. One thing that often blocks a successful contract is a child's activities with his or her friends outside of school. These activities, which are sometimes powerful enough to overwhelm a contract, may range from those that are minor (e.g., eating lunch in a fast food restaurant for a short period of time) to mid-range (e.g., hanging out in a shopping mall for an afternoon) to major (e.g., day parties, drug use, sexual activity, gambling for extended periods of time). By this time in treatment, you should know where your child is during each school day and what he or she is doing.

If problems continue to interfere with the school attendance contracts, then you may need to take more serious steps. These could involve adding stronger rewards for school attendance and stricter punishments for nonattendance (if all parties agree), increasing parent supervision of the youth during the day, and/or legal intervention (e.g., contacting police to break up an illegal drug party). Any legal intervention must be used with caution and you should consider all consequences, including effects on the therapy process. Be sure to consult the therapist.

Another child activity that interferes with school attendance contracts is excessive sleeping in the morning or an inability to get up. This is sometimes worse for children who have been out of school for some time and who are not used to getting up in the morning. For many adolescents, difficulty getting up is normal and temporary. In other cases, the child has a medical problem or a true sleep disorder that requires attention (if this is so, then be sure to consult with a medical doctor or sleep disorders clinic for assessment and treatment). In still other cases, the child has simply stayed up too late and not gotten enough sleep. In a few other cases, the child is feigning fatigue to avoid school.

In the latter two cases, you and the therapist will need to design innovative ways of getting your child out of bed and ready for school. Try setting regular morning and evening routines and bedtimes (see Chapter 6), increasing rewards for rising by a certain time, setting the alarm clock earlier in the morning and constantly reminding your child to get up, and allowing your child to get up later and then walk to school on his or her own. This usually requires some supervision and there is no guarantee the child will get up. Some parents try more drastic measures, but coercive procedures are not recommended. Try to negotiate a solution to the problem with your child and incorporate the solution into the next contract.

At this stage in treatment, your family should be able to define behavior problems. Each family member should be giving his or her opinion about how to define a behavior problem as well as appropriate contract rewards and punishments. If this is not the case, the therapist will repeat procedures described in previous sessions.

Finally, you and your child should have strategies for making up past schoolwork and maintaining academic performance. These strategies may include after-school programs, extra tutoring, supervised homework time, daily report cards, weekly progress reports, rearrangements of class schedules, and/or teacher meetings to collect assignments. Children who like assigned schoolwork and/or do well in school are more likely to stay in their classes. As therapy progresses, you and your child may consider defining different academic problems and solutions and incorporating these into a separate contract.

Peer Refusal Skills Training

By this time in treatment, your child should know how to respond to peers who try to get him or her to skip school. In particular, your child should know specific phrases and conversational techniques that enable him or her to refuse peer pressure without being ridiculed or rejected. In addition, your child should be able to recognize and avoid situations that produce temptations to leave school.

If peer pressure continues to be an issue, however, then the therapist will check your child's refusal skills. If necessary and possible, the therapist will suggest other coping skills such as avoiding certain places at school, not talking to certain peers, and completing homework in the library. In addition, the therapist may use cognitive restructuring procedures to modify any erroneous thoughts your child has about his or her peers and about refusing offers to skip school. For example, children commonly worry that, after turning down offers to skip school, they will lose friends, appear ridiculous, or feel humiliated. If these things are possible, then cognitive restructuring may not be helpful. However, if your child is clearly worried for no legitimate reason when refusing offers to skip school, then cognitive procedures may be helpful (see Chapter 5).

Designing the Contract

If the previous contract involving school attendance was unsuccessful, the therapist will explore any outstanding issues that block the design of an effective contract. If the contract was successful, the therapist will likely ask family members to renew it. However, you may make changes in the contract if everyone agrees. In addition, your family may design a second contract to address other concerns, such as time and activities with friends (see Figure 7.3), oversleeping, and academic problems. In doing so, remember to define each issue specifically and create solutions that are acceptable to everyone.

By this point in treatment, you and your family should be able to design a good contract for a particular problem. You and your family should practice good communication skills during the contract design process. For example, family members could have short one-on-one conversations about possible changes in the upcoming contract. Involve as many family members in this process as possible.

Implementing the Contract

The therapist will ask you to implement the school attendance and/or another contract by following the procedures described previously. By the end of session 6, you and your family should be able to recognize problems sticking to a contract and fix them accordingly. If not, you should discuss this in the therapy session because problems in this area now may lead to problems in the future. Talk about anything (e.g., low motivation) that seems to break down a contract.

Escorting Your Child to School

If you have found it necessary to walk your child from class to class during the school day, be sure that he or she is rewarded for school attendance. In addition, find out whom you should contact if your child leaves school, and how you can gradually withdraw from the escorting situation. Try to rely more on school personnel (e.g., teachers, guidance counselors, attendance officers, hall monitors) to monitor your child and/or give you daily reports about your child. In this way, your child will come to expect that his or her school attendance is always being checked. As much as possible, provide rewards or punishments for school attendance or refusal immediately after the behavior.

In some cases of very persistent school refusal behavior, parents find it quite difficult to constantly follow through on implementing contracts, administering punishments, and/or escorting a child to school and classes. In these cases, some family members feel guilt and frustration and find that their home resembles a battlefield. You should continue to focus on resolving school refusal behavior during the week. However, you also need to maintain family cohesion and fun. In some persistent school refusal cases, for example, it may be necessary for families to set aside treatment procedures on the weekend and enjoy some fun activities together. Because the therapist knows your situation well by this point, consult with him or her about this.

Sample Contract

Privileges	Responsibilities
In exchange for the privilege of spending two hours per school night (6:30-8:30 p.m.) and three hours per weekend night (7:30-10:30 p.m.) with friends between now and the next therapy session, (child) agrees to:	adhere to all aspects of the school attendance contract and inform his or her parent(s) where he or she will be before leaving the house as well as any changes in where he or will be when with his or her friends.
Should (child) not complete this responsibility,	he or she will be required to stay in the house for the next two evenings.
(Child) agrees not to engage in any illegal activity during time spent with friends. Should (child) not complete this responsibility,	this contract is terminated and (child) will be required to stay in the house during the evening until the next therapy session.

(Child) and his or her parents agree to uphold the conditions of this contract and read and initial the contract each day.

Signature of (child) and parents:

____

____ Date: ________________

Figure 7.3.

Homework

Homework assignments after sessions 5–6 may include the following:

- Continue to meet informally as a family 1–2 times between now and the next session. Record your conversations for the therapist if desirable. Discuss aspects of the current contract that are problematic and effective. Practice communication skills as appropriate and desirable.
- Think about problems and potential solutions for the next contract(s). Follow through on procedures to reduce any barriers to contract success.
- Continue to use refusal skills as appropriate.
- Implement the current contract and contact the therapist if necessary.
- Continue to complete the daily logbooks, noting any specific issues or situations that arise during the week.

Sessions 7–8: Completing Treatment

In sessions 7–8, treatment may begin to change in some key ways. First, as your family nears the end of therapy, it is important that the treatment procedures more closely resemble what should be occurring naturally for your child. For example, your child should be going to school on his or her own. In addition, any rewards you give to your child should be made more natural if possible. Also, your family should be setting up contracts more independently of your therapist. *Be careful, though, not to stray too much from treatment procedures that led to your child's return to school.*

Second, treatment procedures may be extended to related problem areas if your child's school refusal behavior is fully or nearly resolved. For example, you may develop contracts for other time periods (e.g., weekends) or behavior problems (e.g., arguing). You and the therapist should not extend these treatment practices, however, until your child's school refusal behavior is under control.

In sessions 7–8, treatment procedures can be finalized and you may wish to talk about ending therapy with the therapist. Also, the therapist may make recommendations to your family about handling child behavior problems and other issues in the near and distant future. The therapist may develop lists of potential pitfalls to avoid, and schedule long-term follow-up contact and booster sessions (see Chapter 8).

Setting Up Times and Places to Negotiate Solutions to Problems

The therapist will review the family meetings that have been taking place at home, especially how family members practiced negotiation and communication. Review your family's list of major problems in this area. If your family continues to fight or have trouble developing contracts, then the therapist will review material from previous sessions to help you improve negotiation or communication.

To ensure that your family has a firm grasp of negotiation and communication skills, the therapist may give you a hypothetical example of a family problem and ask family members to discuss it. The therapist will check the conversations for communication problems and address them as necessary.

If your child is going to school on a near-regular basis, then the family meeting/negotiation/communication process should stay the same. If you have other concerns, then talk to the therapist now. For example, some families become good at talking about school refusal behavior but not other areas. Fighting often continues about marital issues, the child's other behavior problems, extrafamilial activities, finances, and sibling behaviors. If desirable, the therapist will extend negotiation and communication skills training to these other problems. Remember that the chances of relapse will be lower if your family deals with all problems appropriately.

By session 8, the therapist may finalize his or her review of the family meetings that have been taking place at home, and of details about how your family negotiates and communicates with one another. Also, the therapist will give your family a summary of guidelines about speaking with one another appropriately. In doing so, he or she will point out how certain ways of negotiating and communicating helped your child return to school. Remember some basic themes regarding negotiation and communication: simplicity, clarity, respect, and two-way interactions.

Remember that it is easy to slip back into old patterns of communicating once a relatively calm household has been restored. Family members sometimes go back to silence or yelling to make their point. Also, parents sometimes start to take good child behaviors for granted and give punishment (and no rewards) only after severe problems occur. To help counteract this, families should continue to meet regularly and practice the negotiation and communication skills learned in therapy.

Defining the Behavior Problem

The therapist will review with your family the success or failure of the previous contract. As before, he or she will explore any problems that prevented the contract from succeeding. If peer pressure continues to be an issue, then the therapist will check the progress of your child's refusal skills and see if and how they were used. If your family continues to have trouble resolving problems, then the therapist will help your family redefine behavior problems, rewards, and punishments. If necessary, he or she will go back to the point where contracts were simpler and more time-limited. To ensure that your family has a firm grasp of how to define a problem, the therapist may give you a hypothetical example of a vague problem and ask family members to define it. He or she will watch for problems and address them as necessary.

If your child is going to school on a near-regular basis, then your contracting process should stay the same. If you have other concerns, then talk to the therapist now. For example, some families have other problems that are less well-defined than school refusal behavior. Dealing with such problems now will give your family good practice at defining even vague behaviors. List additional problems for the therapist. Examples of behaviors related to school refusal include aggression, noncompliance in other settings, failure to complete homework, social withdrawal, tantrums, refusal to move, general disruptive behavior at home or in class, arguing, and yelling, among others. If these behaviors are a problem, work with the therapist to develop specific definitions now in case you want to use them in the future.

In addition, some parents continue to have vague complaints about their child such as *Joshua lacks self-confidence in school, Sarah shows a lack of respect for others,* or *Andrew's just a bad kid.* Family members should stay away from statements that may be insulting in nature, and restate sentences in a positive and clear manner. In the sentences presented here, for example, the following restatements could be made: *Joshua needs to raise his grades to a "B" level, Sarah and her parents need to interact by speaking in a normal tone of voice,* and *Andrew needs to get more involved in positive extracurricular activities.* Remember that specific, positive statements have more therapeutic value than vague, punishing ones.

By session 8, the therapist and your family may finalize the last set of behavior problem definitions. The therapist will give the family a summary of examples and guidelines about defining key behavior problems. Be sure to make up some sample definitions of common problems in case your family needs them later. Also, the therapist may point out how defining problems in a specific way helped your child's return to school. Remember some basics regarding problem definition: be simple and specific, handle one issue at a time, and allow all members to contribute their own definitions.

Remember as well that it is easy to slip back into old ways of defining problems once a relatively calm household has been restored. In particular, family members sometimes develop a tendency to define a behavior problem specifically (e.g., child needs to be in school) but not completely (for how long?). Be sure to cover all the bases. In addition, keep in mind that your child may need ongoing support to resist peer pressure to skip school. You may go over ways of doing this with the therapist. Finally, remember that a key to stopping school refusal in the future is to help your child maintain his or her academic performance. This may require ongoing contact between you and school officials who can supply daily or weekly report cards.

Designing the Contract

The therapist will ask you to design a new contract to fit your family's current situation. Try to extend the contract timeline (e.g., to 1–2 weeks) if appropriate, and practice communication skills with as many family members as possible during this process. If your family continues to have problems designing contracts, then the therapist will review material from previous sessions to help you.

To ensure that your family has a firm grasp of how to design a contract and communicate appropriately, the therapist may give you a hypothetical example of a vague problem and ask you to design a contract for it. For example, the therapist may give your family a scenario in which the child has recently started to eat in his or her room to stay away from family members. In this example, the therapist may add that increased family fighting makes the child want to eat alone. The therapist will keep the sample problem somewhat vague to get your family to deal with an unclear situation. Remember, you may be dealing with similar unclear situations in the future.

Following this description, your family should start the problem-solving steps taught in the last few sessions. The therapist will observe how you define the problem, communicate with one another, and design a contract. He or she will see if one or a few family members dominates the process, and will step in if your family has problems. Following this "practice time," the therapist will give your family feedback about areas of success and areas that need improvement. Be sure to raise and resolve any remaining issues that might break down effective contracts in the future.

If your child is going to school on a near-regular basis, then the contract design process should stay the same. If you have other concerns, then talk to the therapist now. In addition, draw up sample contracts for related problems in case you want to use them in the future.

By session 8, your family and the therapist may finalize the last set of contracts. The therapist will give your family a summary of examples and guidelines about designing contracts. Remember some basics regarding contract design: agreement by all members, specific and tightly-defined conditions, strong rewards and punishments, limited timeline, signatures, and daily checking by all members. The therapist may point out how specific contracts helped your child return to school.

Remember that, because the contracting process requires time and effort, families sometimes stop using the process once therapy has ended. In particular, families may start to use "oral contracts" where there is general agreement that if the child does "A," the parents will do "B." This method has two main problems. First, families often do not take enough time to carefully design the contract, thus leading to possible loopholes, misinterpretation, and forgetfulness. Second, parents are willing to bribe their child for some good behavior (e.g., school attendance) and not give punishments for some bad behavior (e.g., school refusal). Try to follow the formal contract process that you learned in therapy.

Implementing the Contract

The therapist will ask you to implement this contract following the procedures used previously. If your family continues to have problems implementing contracts, the therapist will review material from previous sessions to help your family follow through. Also, if possible, start to gradually withdraw from going to school with your child if you are currently doing so. Rely more on school officials to monitor your child and/or give you daily reports about him or her.

If your child is going to school on a near-regular basis, then implement the contract in the same way as before. If you have other concerns, then talk to the therapist now. For example, some family members may want to add other behaviors and conditions to the current contract. Be sure not to add too many. If necessary, draw up several small contracts.

By session 8, your family should be implementing the final contracts designed in session with the therapist. Implement these contracts using the procedures described previously. Discuss any remaining problems that interfere with the use of contracts. In particular, the therapist will discuss potential problems that often trouble families once they leave therapy. For example, some families change the contract midway between the start point and end point. If the purpose of this is to close loopholes, that is fine. However, youth often pester their parents to ease up on restrictions and make the contract more favorable to them. Be careful to avoid this. In addition, families sometimes extend a contract indefinitely without discussing it further. This may not consider changes in the child's life, for example, that might make the contract obsolete. Instead, discuss contracts at length at least once a week.

Homework

Homework assignments after sessions 7–8 may include the following:

- Meet formally as a family to discuss issues and problems at least twice per week. Practice communication skills. If a family member wishes to raise a problem, have each family member define it as specifically as possible.
- During these meetings, formulate a contract for a defined problem if appropriate. Implement the contract for a limited time. Discuss aspects of the current contract that are problematic and effective. Try to reduce problems that block contract success.
- Continue to use peer refusal skills and make up schoolwork as appropriate.
- Periodically review lists of pitfalls regarding each of these treatment components given by the therapist.
- Contact the therapist as needed for support, feedback, answers to questions, long-term follow-up, and booster sessions if necessary.

Preventing Slips and Relapse

This chapter defines slips and relapse and gives you a brief overview of how the therapist may help your family prevent your child's return to school refusal behavior. As mentioned in Chapter 1, long-term school refusal behavior may lead to long-term problems as your child ages. As a result, you must work to prevent any backsliding and to address any new problems that do occur as soon as possible. The therapist will likely make more specific recommendations based on your particular case.

Slips Versus Relapse

A slip is a *single* error or some backsliding following treatment. A slip might be a missed school day, one or two days of high stress, short-term avoidance of a particular class, and/or intense but brief acting-out behaviors to stay home from school. Minor slips are not unusual after treatment and are common following long weekends, extended vacations, or, in the case of year-round schools, track breaks.

Relapse, on the other hand, may be defined as a return to old problematic behaviors or substantial backsliding almost to the point when therapy started. Therefore, relapse might involve missing school for several days or weeks, continued high levels of distress, avoidance of many social activities and/or evaluative situations at school, significant misbehaviors to get attention or positive tangible rewards, and/or excessive family conflict over a child's school refusal behavior.

If Slips Occur

If slips occur, and they probably will as your child "tests" your resolve, then return to the therapeutic assignments described in this workbook. In addition, remember the key aspects of the skills that you and your child have learned (see Chapters

4–7). If necessary, review with the therapist some of the key aspects of exposures, relaxation and appropriate breathing, dispute handles and cognitive restructuring exercises, parent commands, forced school attendance, parental firmness and consistency regarding school attendance and refusal, contracts, communication skills, and other techniques in this workbook. It is a good idea to design, with the therapist, "relapse prevention sheets" that contain key reminders of what to do in a given situation. You and your child can then refer to these sheets periodically.

Some general sample reminders for each treatment procedure are listed in Table 8.1. Keep in mind that this is not an exhaustive or even a necessarily pertinent list. The therapist will help you design certain relapse prevention reminders in accordance with your family's particular history and concerns. Specifically, these relapse prevention sheets often involve child-based strategies to cope with certain anxiety-provoking situations, procedures for getting homework and attendance records, house rules, contracts, and appropriate family responses to different child behaviors (e.g., what the family should do if the child runs away from school or avoids class).

Table 8.1. Sample Relapse Prevention Reminders for Families

For children who refused school to avoid objects or situations that cause general distress

1. Practice relaxation and breathing exercises when needed and once per week.
2. Record stressful parts of the day and review them with parents at night.
3. Put aside a safety signal and approach and complete one stressful activity per day.
4. Practice self-reinforcement when appropriate exposure occurs.

For children who refused school to escape painful social and/or evaluative situations

1. Keep a journal of automatic thoughts during stressful times of the day.
2. Practice changing thoughts to coping, helpful ones when necessary.
3. Approach and have a five-minute conversation with three people per day.
4. Participate in one extracurricular activity per semester.

For children who refused school for attention

1. Review commands given to the child daily.
2. Administer consequences for misbehaviors as soon as they occur in different settings and at different times; work through tantrums in preparing the child for school.
3. Maintain the regularity and predictability of the child's morning routine.
4. Allow the child to ask one question on one topic per hour.

For children who refused school to pursue tangible rewards outside of school

1. Monitor the child's school attendance on a daily basis.
2. Contact teachers or other school officials once per week regarding the child's academic work.
3. Schedule one family problem-solving meeting per week.
4. Develop and implement a contract twice per month.

Don't be discouraged when slips happen. Some family members make the mistake of thinking that, if the child refuses school again or becomes somewhat more anxious, then the entire therapy process was wasted. This is not true. Slips are usually the result of relaxed efforts and not incompetence on your part or your child's part. Instead, try to view the situation as a challenging one that will help you and your child practice the skills learned in therapy.

If slips continue for a while, or if you and your child are becoming increasingly frustrated about renewed school refusal behavior, then contact the therapist. In fact, the therapist may recommend that you stay in occasional telephone contact as needed after your family ends formal treatment. This is a way of discussing progress as well as any new issues that arise that contribute to slips (e.g., changes in class schedule, academic problems, other stressors). However, try not to become too dependent on the therapist for feedback. Instead, try to initially solve any new problems or slips based on skills that you and your child learned in therapy.

If Relapse Occurs

In situations where slips are becoming too frequent, however, and your child seems to be relapsing into regular school refusal behavior, then be sure to discuss this with the therapist. He or she may be able to provide some feedback on what to do or schedule you and/or your family for additional treatment sessions. *Do not wait until the following school year to address relapse.* Some parents, if their child starts refusing school again in the late spring, become discouraged and simply wait out the school year or believe there is no point in addressing school refusal behavior at so late a time. However, if the child successfully refuses school during the late spring, this may mean that he or she will be out of school for several months (i.e., during spring and summer). This will make getting the child back to school in the fall a much harder task. A better strategy would be to reintegrate your child back into school in the late spring (with, perhaps, the therapist's help) and then pursue summer classes or other strategies to keep your child active and knowing that you will react to school refusal behavior whenever it occurs.

If relapse occurs, don't be discouraged. Relapses do happen, especially in more severe cases of school refusal behavior. However, perseverance is often as important a quality as any of the techniques described in this workbook. In other words, the more you and your child keep trying to resolve the problem, the more long-term success you and your child are likely to see.

Preventing Slips and Relapse

There are techniques that you, your child, and the therapist may engage in to try to prevent slips and relapse even before they begin. Some of these techniques can take place as therapy is ending, and others may take place at some time in the future.

Photographs and the Return-to-School Storybook

One method of relapse prevention involves taking photographs during in vivo exposure or desensitization practices. This can be especially effective for children who previously had a lot of distress or social anxiety about school, but may also be useful for children who refused school for attention or tangible rewards and who may be in school for the first time on their own. Whatever the reason, photographs are a way to reinforce your child for his or her accomplishments. You can display the pictures in a prominent place in your home (e.g., refrigerator, bedroom door), much as you would your child's report card, drawing, or other personal accomplishment. In this way, your child can be continually reminded of his or her progress.

Another family-oriented activity to reinforce your child's progress is the creation of a poster, journal, or storybook of your child's accomplishments using the photographs of your child's exposures. Helpful photographs include the child sitting at his or her school desk, talking with the teacher, interacting with friends, riding the school bus, and giving an oral report in front of the class. For each of the photographs, help your child write a caption or description of the scene, including what he or she is thinking, feeling, and doing in the photograph. Combining the photographs with your child's own written words serves as a creative and personal reminder and reinforcer of special moments in your child's therapy program.

Commercial

Another relapse prevention technique is the commercial. Dr. Philip Kendall is the originator of this unique and highly successful idea for preventing slips and relapse (Kendall, et al., 1992). Specifically, the therapist may ask your child's help in producing a video "commercial" aimed at teaching other children how to overcome the problem of school refusal behavior. This is often done toward the end of treatment. In making the commercial, the therapist will serve as the "director" of the project, but your child is the expert on the subject and star of the show. By enlisting your child as an expert in how to overcome school refusal, your child's self-esteem and feelings of empowerment are boosted.

The therapist will guide your child's performance, ensuring that all the key elements of his or her treatment are presented in the video. For example, if your child's treatment involved relaxation or breathing techniques, demonstrations of these methods will be placed in the video. Your child will be coached to describe the three parts of an anxious feeling (physical feelings, thoughts, behavior) and the ways in which these three components build upon each other during stressful situations. Cognitive methods (STOP; Silverman & Kurtines, 1992) might also be described, with relevant examples presented by your child. If a portable camcorder is available, the therapist will ask you to videotape your child conducting key in vivo STIC tasks such as riding on the school bus or eating in the cafeteria.

Some children devise very creative scripts for these videos. For example, one child acted as the "game show host" as he quizzed family members and the therapist on various techniques for overcoming negative emotions. Another child acted as a reporter who "investigated" the problem of school refusal in which she uncovered negative thoughts and the "aggravations from avoidance." Even though the video is developed as a way to teach other children how to overcome their problem, your child keeps the video for his or her exclusive use. In this way, you can periodically play the video to remind your child of the program and to prevent setbacks during times of high stress or vulnerability (e.g., before the start of school, during standardized testing times).

Structured Activities Outside the Home

Long breaks from school, such as summer vacation or the December holidays, can provide enough time for a child to "slip" backwards to inappropriate habits and anxieties. Children who relapse may have greater tendencies to experience negative emotions and anxiety. Typically, the plans and procedures taught in therapy are forgotten or put aside during this time. There is the tendency to want to "leave well enough alone" and not continue to practice the procedures and skills learned in therapy. To prevent relapse, keep your child as much as possible on a regular "school" schedule during holidays. This means regular waking times and routines in the morning and a regular bedtime at night. This assures that your child's sleep-wake cycle stays within normal limits and that he or she gets a sufficient amount of sleep. During the summer, try to start your child's normal "school" schedule about three weeks prior to the start of school. For children who refused school in the past for tangible rewards, gradual restrictions on curfew and time spent with friends may need to start at this time. In this way, your child's day can start to mimic what will need to happen when school starts.

During summer vacation, try to have your child spend some portion of each weekday outside the home in an organized activity with other children and adults. For example, day camps, volunteer programs, sporting activities, youth groups, and library programs can give your child contact with people outside the family. This will allow your child to continue to practice and refine his or her anxiety management skills. In addition, especially for attention-seeking children, more independent activities will help prevent backsliding to dependency on you for moment-to-moment support. If there are no structured programs available in your area, organize other parents in your community to form play groups or activity programs that can be rotated from house to house. Again, this will gently "force" your child to remain in contact with others and will serve as a natural desensitization and exposure process. This will give children with separation anxiety practice at leaving primary caretakers and functioning well on their own.

Booster Sessions

Some therapists and schools will provide "booster" programs for children who had previously refused to attend school. Booster sessions may be provided in individual or group format. These sessions are usually scheduled at high pressure times of the year, such as early August before the start of school, during a mid-semester break, or during exam periods. The purpose of the booster program is to review skills and discuss any potential problems that your child worries may occur. By anticipating these problems and intervening before they occur, your child is more likely to successfully re-enter school and engage in school life. Booster programs may be particularly important for children making a transition from elementary to middle school or from middle school to high school. Transition times are difficult for children who have had a history of school refusal, anxiety, or depression. Booster programs are usually structured, short-term, and highly individualized to meet the child's needs.

Introduction to a New School

Because many children have trouble coping with changing social and academic scenarios, especially when advancing to a new (e.g., middle, high) school, it is important to allow them to explore the new school building before classes begin. You can do this a few days before school starts with cooperation from the child's new school counselor. Be careful, however, that your child doesn't view the counselor and his/her office as simply a safety signal. Of special interest are the location of lockers, specific classrooms, cafeteria, libraries, gymnasiums, main and guidance offices, exits, and settings for getting on and off the school bus. Maps are also helpful, but encourage your child to be as independent as possible. Because children with previous school refusal behavior often worry about getting lost and looking foolish, taking them on a tour of their new school building may serve to diminish anticipatory anxiety, increase self-efficacy, and prevent relapse. Your child should also receive information on school-based social and sporting groups that he or she is eligible to join that semester. Gently encourage your child to become socially active in these groups.

Children With Chronic School Refusal Behavior

For children with chronic school refusal behavior, relapse prevention is quite challenging. Follow-up in these cases will generally need to be more frequent and intensive than follow-up for cases involving acute school refusal behavior. Relapse prevention in chronic cases is likely to depend more on reduced family conflict, reduced child noncompliance and disruptive behavior, changes in parent attitudes, the child's participation in extracurricular activities and development of appropriate social contacts, continued motivation to attend school, and ongoing medical interventions, if applicable. As a result, you may need to be vigilant about slips in many more different areas than just those specifically related to school refusal behavior. You and the therapist may also remain in close contact following the end of formal treatment.

Keep in mind as well that, because children with chronic school refusal behavior are often placed in alternative or part-time curricular programs, you should be aware of any upcoming changes that could interrupt attendance. For example, a school district with financial difficulties may be forced to eliminate an after-school program that your child was attending. In this case, you may have to make alternative arrangements for attending classes during the day, evening, or summer. In addition, you may find that your child is showing new behaviors (e.g., substance abuse, depression) that could interfere with school attendance. In this case, contacting the therapist for feedback, rescheduling therapy sessions, or pursuing treatment with another specialist are possible options.

Overall, relapse prevention for children with chronic school refusal behavior will depend on a close monitoring of attendance and related behaviors for at least several months. As a result, you should maintain a healthy relationship with the therapist and school officials (e.g., teachers, attendance officers) who can help you identify and address problems as early as possible. In this way, you can lower the chances of relapse to school refusal behavior.

Some Final Comments

Dealing with school refusal behavior can often be a trying experience for both parents and children. This workbook tries to provide guidelines for identifying school refusal behaviors and addressing them in a timely fashion. Hopefully, you have found the procedures in this workbook useful. We invite any comments you may have about these procedures. We have been helping families for several years and have found that, with the assistance and information described in this workbook, children and their parents have become their own best experts.

References

Beck, A. T., Rush, A. J., Shaw, B. F., & Emery, G. (1979). *Cognitive therapy of depression.* New York: Guilford Press.

Kendall, P. C., Chansky, T. E., Kane, M. T., Kim, R. S., Kortlander, E., Ronan, K. R., Sessa, F. M., & Siqueland, L. (1992). *Anxiety disorders in youth: Cognitive-behavioral interventions.* Boston: Allyn and Bacon.

Ollendick, T. H., & Cerny, J. A. (1981). *Clinical behavior therapy with children.* New York: Plenum Press.

Silverman, W.K., & Kurtines, W.M. (1996). *Anxiety and phobic disorders: A pragmatic approach.* New York: Plenum Press.

Appendix

School Refusal Assessment Scale (Child)

Your name: ______________________________

Date: ______________________________

Please circle the answer that best answers the following questions:

1. How often do you have trouble going to school because you are afraid of something in the school building (for example, a fire alarm, room, etc.)?

Never		Seldom	Half the Time		Usually	Always
0	1	2	3	4	5	6

2. Do you have trouble speaking with the other kids at school?

Never		Seldom	Half the Time		Usually	Always
0	1	2	3	4	5	6

3. Do you often do things to upset or annoy your family?

Never		Seldom	Half the Time		Usually	Always
0	1	2	3	4	5	6

4. How often do you go out of the house when not in school during the week (Monday to Friday)?

Never		Seldom	Half the Time		Usually	Always
0	1	2	3	4	5	6

5. Are you afraid of the teachers or others at school?

Never		Seldom	Half the Time		Usually	Always
0	1	2	3	4	5	6

6. Do you feel embarrassed or scared in front of other people at school?

Never		Seldom	Half the Time		Usually	Always
0	1	2	3	4	5	6

7. How often do you feel that you would rather be with your parents than attend school?

Never		Seldom	Half the Time		Usually	Always
0	1	2	3	4	5	6

Figure A.1.

8. Do you ever talk to or see other people when not in school during the week (Monday to Friday)?

Never		Seldom	Half the Time		Usually	Always
0	1	2	3	4	5	6

9. Do you feel more nervous with your friends at school than with your friends somewhere else (e.g., at a party or at home)?

Never		Seldom	Half the Time		Usually	Always
0	1	2	3	4	5	6

10. Do you have trouble making friends?

Never		Seldom	Half the Time		Usually	Always
0	1	2	3	4	5	6

11. Do you ever think about your parents or family when in school or when they are away from you?

Never		Seldom	Half the Time		Usually	Always
0	1	2	3	4	5	6

12. Do you enjoy doing different things when not in school during the week (Monday to Friday)?

Never		Seldom	Half the Time		Usually	Always
0	1	2	3	4	5	6

13. Do you feel scared about school when you think about it on Saturday and Sunday?

Never		Seldom	Half the Time		Usually	Always
0	1	2	3	4	5	6

14. Do you often stay away from places where you would have to talk to someone?

Never		Seldom	Half the Time		Usually	Always
0	1	2	3	4	5	6

15. Do you ever refuse to go to school in order to be with your parents?

Never		Seldom	Half the Time		Usually	Always
0	1	2	3	4	5	6

16. Do you ever skip school because it's more fun to be out of school?

Never		Seldom	Half the Time		Usually	Always
0	1	2	3	4	5	6

Figure A.1.

School Refusal Assessment Scale (Child) *continued*

ANA	ESE	AGB	PTR
1. ________	2. ________	3. ________	4. ________
5 ________	6. ________	7. ________	8. ________
9. ________	10. ________	11. ________	12. ________
13. ________	14. ________	15. ________	16. ________
Total score =________	________	________	________
Mean score =________	________	________	________

Figure A.1.

School Refusal Assessment Scale (Parent)

Your child's name: ______________________________

Date: ______________________________

Please circle the answer that best answers the following questions:

1. Does your child seem extremely fearful of something at or within the school building (for example, a fire alarm, room, etc.)?

Never		Seldom	Half the Time		Usually	Always
0	1	2	3	4	5	6

2. Does your child have problems speaking with the other kids at school?

Never		Seldom	Half the Time		Usually	Always
0	1	2	3	4	5	6

3. Does your child seem to upset or annoy you to gain attention?

Never		Seldom	Half the Time		Usually	Always
0	1	2	3	4	5	6

4. Does your child go out of the house when not in school during the week (Monday to Friday)?

Never		Seldom	Half the Time		Usually	Always
0	1	2	3	4	5	6

5. Does your child seem frightened of the teachers or others at school?

Never		Seldom	Half the Time		Usually	Always
0	1	2	3	4	5	6

6. Does your child say to you that he/she feels uncomfortable or embarrassed in front of other people at school?

Never		Seldom	Half the Time		Usually	Always
0	1	2	3	4	5	6

7. How often does your child wish to be with you or your spouse rather than attend school?

Never		Seldom	Half the Time		Usually	Always
0	1	2	3	4	5	6

Figure A.2.

8. Does your child often speak to or see other people when not in school during the week (Monday to Friday)?

Never		Seldom	Half the Time		Usually	Always
0	1	2	3	4	5	6

9. Does your child seem more nervous with his/her friends when in school than with his/her friends somewhere else (e.g., at a party or at home)?

Never		Seldom	Half the Time		Usually	Always
0	1	2	3	4	5	6

10. Does your child say that he/she has trouble making friends?

Never		Seldom	Half the Time		Usually	Always
0	1	2	3	4	5	6

11. Does your child say that he/she thinks of you often when you are away?

Never		Seldom	Half the Time		Usually	Always
0	1	2	3	4	5	6

12. Does your child enjoy doing various activities when not in school during the week (Monday to Friday)?

Never		Seldom	Half the Time		Usually	Always
0	1	2	3	4	5	6

13. Does your child seem scared about school on the weekends?

Never		Seldom	Half the Time		Usually	Always
0	1	2	3	4	5	6

14. Does your child seem to avoid social situations where talking to others is likely?

Never		Seldom	Half the Time		Usually	Always
0	1	2	3	4	5	6

15. Does your child ever refuse to attend school just to be with you or your spouse?

Never		Seldom	Half the Time		Usually	Always
0	1	2	3	4	5	6

16. Does your child skip school because he/she has more fun outside of school?

Never		Seldom	Half the Time		Usually	Always
0	1	2	3	4	5	6

Figure A.2.

School Refusal Assessment Scale (Parent) *continued*

ANA	ESE	AGB	PTR
1. ______	2. ______	3. ______	4. ______
5 ______	6. ______	7. ______	8. ______
9. ______	10. ______	11. ______	12. ______
13. ______	14. ______	15. ______	16. ______
Total score = ______	______	______	______
Mean score = ______	______	______	______

Figure A.2.

Child's Daily Logbook

Your name: ____

Please rate the following every day on a 0–10 scale where 0 = none, 2 = mild, 4 = moderate, 6 = marked, 8 = severe, and 10 = extreme (for younger children: 0–10 scale where 0 = none, 2–3 is a little, 5 is some, 7–8 is much, and 10 is very much).

Date	Anxiety	Depression	Distress
________	________	________	________
________	________	________	________
________	________	________	________
________	________	________	________
________	________	________	________
________	________	________	________
________	________	________	________
________	________	________	________

Please list any problems you have had at home or school since the last session:

Figure A.3.

Parent's Daily Logbook

Your child's name: ______________________________

Please rate your child's behaviors every day on a 0–10 scale where 0 = none, 2 = mild, 4 = moderate, 6 = marked, 8 = severe, and 10 = extreme.

Date	Anxiety	Depression	Distress	Noncompliance	Disruption
______	______	______	______	______	______
______	______	______	______	______	______
______	______	______	______	______	______
______	______	______	______	______	______
______	______	______	______	______	______
______	______	______	______	______	______
______	______	______	______	______	______
______	______	______	______	______	______

Please list any specific problems your child has had at home or school since the last session:

Please list the amount of school time your child has missed since the last session:

Figure A.4.

Anxiety and Avoidance Hierarchy

Problem:

Situations or Places That Scare Me!	Anxiety Rating	Avoidance Rating
1.		
2.		
3.		
4.		
5.		
6.		
7.		
8.		
9.		
10.		

Figure A.5. **Anxiety and Avoidance Hierarchy**

Feelings Thermometer

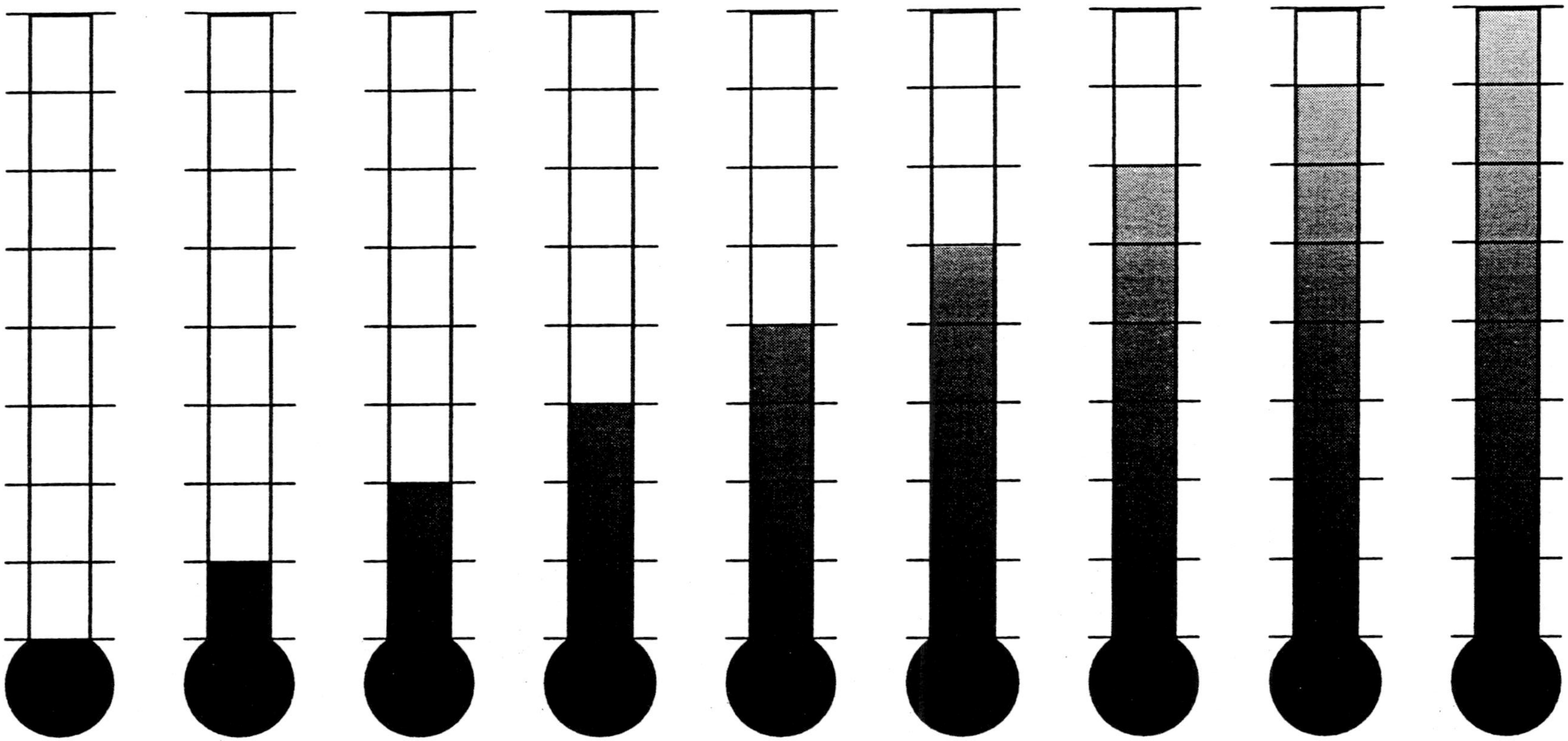

0	2	4	6	8
Not at all	A little bit	Some	A lot	Very, very much

Figure A.6.

Contract

Privileges	Responsibilities
General	
Specific	

(Child) and his or her parents agree to uphold the conditions of this contract and read and initial the contract each day.

Signature of (child) and parents:

____

____ Date: ______________

Figure A.7.

9 780158 132259